Life and Fire of Love

Life and Fire of Love

Prayer and its presuppositions

by

HERBERT M. WADDAMS

Canon Residentiary of Canterbury Cathedral

LONDON

S·P·C·K

1964

First published in 1964
by S.P.C.K.
Holy Trinity Church
Marylebone Road
London N.W.1

Made and printed in Great Britain by
William Clowes and Sons, Limited, London and Beccles

TO MY WIFE

Contents

CONTENTS

Acknowledgements

It will be obvious to anyone who reads this book that the author is indebted to many writers, past and present, for inspiration and instruction. The use of their ideas and the recognition of the illumination which they have brought is the best tribute he can pay to them. On the practical side he is particularly grateful to Mrs Ruth Fahrig of Ottawa who, in the midst of a busy family life, kindly put the whole work into typescript, and also to Miss Veronica Ruffer who read it and gave useful advice.

Thanks are also due to the following for permission to include copyright material:

Beauchesne et ses Fils, Paris: *LUI et Moi: Entretiens Spirituels*, by Gabrielle Bossis.

Burns and Oates, Ltd, and Harper and Row, Publishers, Inc.: *The English Mystical Tradition*, by Dom David Knowles.

Burns and Oates, Ltd, the Right Reverend Abbot, the Abbey of Gethsemani, Kentucky, and Farrar, Straus and Co., Inc.: *Seeds of Contemplation* and *Thoughts in Solitude*, by Thomas Merton.

Burns and Oates, Ltd, and the Newman Press: *The Complete Works of St John of the Cross* and *The Treatise on Prayer* of St Peter of Alcantara.

Cambridge University Press: *John Cassian*, by Owen Chadwick.

James Clarke and Co., Ltd: *The Mystical Theology of the Eastern Church*, by Vladimir Lossky.

J. M. Dent and Sons, Ltd: *The Mystical Element of Religion*, by F. von Hügel.

Faber and Faber, Ltd: *Early Fathers from the Philokalia*, by E. Kadloubovsky (tr. G. E. H. Palmer).

The Faith Press, Ltd: *Straight Course to God*, by Dom Augustine Morris.

The Faith Press, Ltd, and Editions du Seuil: *Introduction à l'Etude de Grégoire Palamas*, by Jean Meyendorff.

ACKNOWLEDGEMENTS

Harper and Row, Publishers, Inc: *Pastoral Counseling*, by Carroll A. Wise; *Christian Perfection*, by François Fénelon (ed. Charles F. Whiston).

James Clarke and Co., Ltd: *The Mystical Theology of the Eastern Church*, Vladimir Lossky.

Longmans, Green and Co., Ltd: *Some Principles of Moral Theology*, by K. E. Kirk; *Speculum Animae*, by W. R. Inge; *The Letters of Evelyn Underhill*. (The last-named quoted also by courtesy of the David McKay Company, Inc.)

Methuen and Co., Ltd: *The Revelations of the Divine Love*, by Lady Julian.

A. R. Mowbray and Co., Ltd: *The Spiritual Exercises of St Ignatius Loyola*, ed. W. H. Longridge; *St Bernard on the Love of God*.

Routledge and Kegan Paul, Ltd: *Waiting on God*, by Simone Weil.

The S.C.M. Press, Ltd, and Harper and Row, Publishers, Inc.: *The Meaning of Persons*, by Paul Tournier.

Sheed and Ward, Ltd: *Spiritual Letters*, by Dom John Chapman.

Sheed and Ward, Ltd, and Sheed and Ward, Inc.: *Moral Problems Now* (published in the U.S.A. under the title *Counseling the Catholic: Modern Techniques and Emotional Conflicts*), George Hagmaier, C.S.P., and Robert Gleason, S.J.; *The Interior Castle*, from *The Complete Works of Saint Teresa*, Vol. II, translated and edited by E. Allison Peers from the critical edition of P. Silverio de Santa Terera, C.D.

John M. Watkins: *The Scale of Perfection*, by Walter Hilton, ed. Evelyn Underhill.

Biblical quotations are taken from *The New English Bible: New Testament*, copyright 1961, Oxford and Cambridge University Presses.

Apologies are offered to any inadvertently omitted.

Love

Love bade me welcome; yet my soul drew back,
        Guiltie of dust and sinne.
But quick-ey'd Love, observing me grow slack
        From my first entrance in,
Drew nearer to me, sweetly questioning,
        If I lack'd any thing.
"A guest," I answer'd, "worthy to be here:"
        Love said, "You shall be he."
"I the unkinde, ungratefull? Ah my deare,
        I cannot look on thee."
Love took my hand, and smiling did reply,
        "Who made the eyes but I?"
"Truth Lord, but I have marr'd them: let my shame
        Go where it doth deserve."
"And know you not," sayes Love, "who bore the blame?"
        "My deare, then I will serve."
"You must sit down," sayes Love, "and taste my meat."
        So I did sit and eat.

GEORGE HERBERT

The Christian Life

1

Introductory

This is a book about one aspect of the Christian life. It deals with a subject which is sometimes called ascetical theology. The word "ascetical" carries various meanings, but here it is used in its proper sense, directly derived from its Greek original *askesis*, to mean training, practice, exercise, and related activities and attitudes which are needed for growth in the life which God wants men to live.

To this it may be objected that there are far too many books on this subject already, and that it is most unlikely that the present author can improve on the many excellent books which already exist. The writer is fain to agree that there is much force in this objection. Nevertheless he hopes that there is a place for an approach which is a little different from that which is usually followed.

There are two main sources from which enlightenment on ascetical theology may be drawn. The first is the New Testament and the second is the teaching and practice of the Church through the ages. The latter is an immense quarry which it is impossible for one person adequately to explore, still less exhaust; yet it must be considered with the New Testament as the place where we see the principles and teaching of the Gospel worked out under the guidance of the Holy Spirit in the life of the fellowship which itself sprang out of the Gospel, the Church.

Because of the immense variety of the material, writers on this topic tend to confine themselves to one or two spiritual writers, or at best to follow one fairly coherent tradition. This method has its advantages, but it suffers too from drawbacks. One danger is that such an approach may import into a consideration of the spiritual life the divisions of the Churches as they show themselves in outward organization. Yet this is an area where these divisions ought not to be allowed to intrude, for it is the place where those who are living in union with God, whatever Church they belong to, are united by his love in a deep and unbreakable bond.

In our century more and more Christians realize that, in loyalty to the Gospel itself, they must look for ties which unite them to other Christians of different traditions through seeking for that unity which Christ bestowed on his disciples and for which he prayed so earnestly before his passion, as we read in the fifteenth, sixteenth, and seventeenth chapters of St John's gospel. It has long been my sincere conviction that a closer and more careful study of one another's Christian traditions is likely to be one of the most fruitful ways forward to a greater understanding, fellowship, and charity among Christian people. Indeed, it was because he penetrated below the surface divisions to the underlying spiritual truths that the late Abbé Paul Couturier of Lyons made such a deep impact on the practice of prayer for Christian unity, seeing it, as he did, as the outcome of sanctification, of being made holy. In other words, it is only as Christians are more and more submitted to the will of God that unity among themselves can even be properly conceived, let alone achieved.

The approach, therefore, of this book is broad, recognizing the spirit of God at work in Protestants as well as in Catholics and Orthodox, finding among them all the same basic teaching about the life of prayer and surrender to God, and trying to distinguish the authentic Christian note as distinct from the small aberrations which from time to time may be found in the writers concerned. For all, even the saints, were to a certain extent inhibited in their powers of expression, both by their own mental and physical powers and also by the climate of thought of the time in which they wrote. This latter point ought always to be remembered. Anyone who is writing for his contemporaries inevitably writes in the thought-forms which are the common currency of his generation. It is, therefore, always vital, as with the Creeds, to distinguish between what is the temporary and passing fashion in which the thoughts are clothed, and the reality of the thoughts themselves.

Another tendency among writers on ascetical theology, especially perhaps in the Roman Catholic Church, is to overdo the categorization of the study. It is a common human desire to have everything nicely docketed and tidily arranged, for by this means the student gains a feeling of control over his material. But here too is a danger, since there are some subjects which can only be impoverished by such categories. The Christian life is one of these. The spiritual life of Christians is as various as humanity itself: just as creation reflects the infinite richness and variety of the Creator, so does the human spirit in all its manifestations. If we try to compose a scheme into which everyone fits we shall inevitably be making smaller the great gifts of God, since we are cutting them down to size—the size of our minds. Systematization, therefore, has to be carefully controlled.

Of course there is much value in trying to deduce general truths from all the details which are available, and such truths are most valuable. Writers who are systematic in the treatment of the prayer life often put us in their debt by making clearer the importance of such general truths. But our gratitude should not permit us to approve of a system in which everything must be docketed, and which may have the effect of removing the spontaneity from the spiritual life.

The virtues of spontaneity can easily be overestimated, but it is a basic necessity in the spiritual life because it avoids being tied down by a strict rule or method. The great method of prayer is to have none, as St Jeanne de Chantal wrote.[1] The motions of the Holy Spirit in the soul must have free play and not be obstructed by the plans and methods which we have adopted for our own advance. For it is a prime principle of the spiritual life that progress comes only by the Holy Spirit, the action of God in the soul, and cannot be acquired by any particular method or trick.

But on the other hand some rules are needed, as will be evident later. Spontaneity does not mean that there is no need for discipline and order in the spiritual life, for these are indispensable for all

[1] *Œuvres*, vol. ii, p. 337.

Christians. But it does mean that union with God and advance in knowledge and love of him cannot be obtained by hitting on the right method, but can only come by the power of his Holy Spirit. The relation of method to prayer may perhaps be likened to that between the technique of writing music and the beauty of inspiration. The discipline of learning and practising the rules of harmony are an indispensable preliminary to good composing, but they do not themselves provide beautiful music. The most accomplished technique merely provides the necessary raw material through which the inspiration of beautiful music may be expressed. But the inspiration is from elsewhere—from God.

The method which we shall follow will take account of the systematic treatment of prayer in the Christian life but without being bound by any one system. We shall attempt to bring together the principles of the prayer life which we find in the New Testament, in the life of the Church, and in the writings of the great masters so as to distil from them the basic truths about its growth. This will involve selection, and selection is bound to be arbitrary. Out of the immense amount of material, only small sections can be examined, but an effort will be made to make those small sections fairly represent the writers from which they come in the sense that they do not misrepresent any important principle of their teaching, but throw some positive light upon it.

Our aim will be practical, not merely theoretical. The subjects chosen for discussion are those on which ordinary men and women need guidance, and on which there is often misunderstanding and confusion. They will be considered on broad lines without the minor variations, which would need a longer and more academic approach than is possible for the present writer.

I follow the example of many writers on this subject and add that what is here written is subject to the judgement of the Church, in which alone the fullness of the Christian life can be lived. I pray that none may be led astray by any careless or inadequate word, and that, by the grace of the Holy Spirit of God, light may be given to some who have the patience and persistence to read what follows.

2

The Spiritual Life

It would be safe to guess that a large majority of those reading the phrase "the spiritual life" take it to mean the life of prayer, or some activities which are connected with acts of piety. In doing so they are merely accepting the common meaning of the words without recognizing that they have become debased, and that their full meaning is much wider.

"Spiritual" is a word which has come to mean something contrasted with "material"—something which ministers of religion or Eastern mystics talk and write about, but which has little to do with the normal everyday life of men and women, especially in Western civilization. There is a dichotomy between the words "spiritual" and "material", which is encouraged by the modern use of "materialist" to refer to attitudes which deny the reality of anything beyond matter. More confusion is caused by the fact these words are also used with different shades of meanings.

Dr Leonard Hodgson has some wise remarks on the use of these terms. He writes:

> I am quite sure in my own mind that when we use these words "spiritual" and "material" we should not regard them as meaning two different kinds of stuff which are put together in a kind of amalgam, but as referring to different stages in the process of our coming existence. Everything which functions according to forces acting upon it and through it, as at the subhuman level in the evolutionary process, is behaving materially. But when we act consciously, determinately, making up our minds to do something and doing it, then we are acting as spiritual beings.[1]

[1] *Church and Sacraments in Divided Christendom*, p. 24.

This has implications which we ought to look at. The distinction between spiritual and material which is ordinarily made by people often depends on the idea of the immortal soul inhabiting a temporary and mortal body, so that the human personality is thought to be made up of different bits, for the time being stuck together and intimately united, but not permanently so. Thus at the death of the body the soul is said to live on and to grow during a period of purification until it reaches its fullness of life, or is looked after in some undefined way until at the general resurrection it is given a new body and once more becomes a full personality.

But if we are to follow Dr Hodgson this would not seem to be a proper way of approach. We might accept his words as meaning that our process of existence begins as merely material, and then becomes spiritual in the way he describes, and at death sloughs off its physical body as a chrysalis does its skin so as to release the butterfly, the only difference being that the butterfly is physical and the soul is not. But we are then faced with the Christian teaching of the final resurrection of the body and the reuniting of spirit and matter in a condition where both will be fully one and both entirely submitted to the will of God in fellowship with him. We see the importance of the body retaining a permanent place in Christian thought, and that the body should not be considered something inferior, to be done away with at some stage of progressing to higher things.

There is, however, little doubt that the idea that the physical is inferior, or even evil, has left strong traces in Christian thought at almost all times. But the idea has no warrant in the Old and New Testaments and it is not in accord with the teaching either of our Lord, or of St Paul, or of the other New Testament writers. The biblical approach to matter is enshrined in the early words of Genesis: "And God saw everything that he had made, and behold, it was very good." The message of the Gospel is a message of the redemption of the whole created world and not merely teaching about the spiritual in an anti-material or non-material sense.

These general considerations have an important bearing on the

Christian life and the life of prayer, for in some writers on the subject it is plain that the material and physical are primarily seen as obstacles to, instead of as instruments of, the spiritual life. The direct result of such a conception is that extreme mortification and subjection of the flesh is thought to be an indispensable preliminary of any spiritual growth. Such is not the teaching of the best writers who maintain that too much emphasis on mortification and self-abnegation of the flesh can have bad spiritual results. Balance in self-discipline, as in everything else to do with the life of the Christian, is a prime need.

The spiritual life, then, is not a life different from and separated from the material life and the life of our physical body. It is the life in which material things become what God intended them to be, instead of being the means of alienation from God. Christianity is a materialistic religion in that it stresses the importance of the material, every part of it, as the God-given means of making our lives what he wants them to be. It is not possible to live the life of God and at the same time to deny the goodness of the gift of physical life which he has given us. When through that physical life shines the love of God, then the fullness of spiritual life on earth begins to be known.

But, of course, the physical does very easily become an obstacle to the spiritual, as we can readily see by looking at the people among whom we live and by examining the history of our own attempts and failures to reach the level of true service to God. There is a fundamental spiritual truth, which can hardly too often be repeated or learned, namely, that every event, and every occurrence in the life of man, has two sides: on the one side it is an opportunity for finding, serving, and revealing God; but on the other it is a temptation to put something else in the place of God, in every case the satisfaction of some physical, mental, or spiritual enjoyment of man.

This two-sided aspect of life runs through everything known to man, from the simplest physical need, like food, to the highest spiritual flights, like the love of God. Food is necessary, it is good, it is needed for bodily and for spiritual health, it is provided by God for these purposes. But if food is made an end in itself instead of an instrument of God's will, if a man becomes a glutton, the food becomes the very opposite thing to that for which it was intended—it becomes an obstacle to God's will instead of an instrument of it. On the higher planes of prayer the love for God which a Christian wants to exercise can subtly be changed into a love for self, if prayer becomes an exercise which is mainly concerned with the effect on the person who prays, rather than submission to the will of God. In this way even humility can be turned into pride by posing as a cause for self-satisfaction.

The basic fact seems to be that God says to man: "Here is so much raw material for body, mind, and spirit. You have to make use of it. What you do with it will determine your own future and happiness. It is essential to your life: you cannot live without using it. There is no opting out for anyone who claims to be human. But there is only one way in which it can serve to bring you to your own highest possibilities and to the fullness of happiness for ever, that it should be used to fulfil perfectly the plan for which it was made. Any other use brings with it its own condemnation and eternal frustration."

But he goes on to add that he will not interfere with our free choice. Such freedom is an indispensable part of making good. More than this, we have to exercise this freedom in conditions which make it difficult to use it aright, because it has been so much misused in the past. The result is that a great part of the raw material which has been put at man's disposal is already being put to the service of anti-God and selfish interests. The whole weight, therefore, of the world puts pressure on us to use the material in the wrong way. We want material things for ourselves; our mental accomplishments make us think that we can do all we want; and our spiritual attitudes are that we are self-sufficient.

But God has shown us how, in spite of all this overpowering wrongness, the raw material can be wrested from the power of evil and turned to the use which God intended it to have. The life of Jesus showed in his person that perfect and self-sacrificing love could bring good out of evil and once more make the physical, mental, and spiritual raw material the embodiment of God's will and God's love.

This is what the spiritual life is all about. And it is because of the immensity and complication of evil that attempts to categorize and to arrange the spiritual life into tidy rules and regulations is never completely successful. Of course such efforts can often bring some illumination which helps us to see the truth more clearly, but they can never adequately deal with the immense varieties of situations which life brings before us nor with the incredible varieties of human personalities which have to deal with those situations. Rule of thumb is never more dangerous than in the spiritual life, although there have been fine persons who have overlooked its dangers.

There is much in the experiences of the saints and ordinary men and women of Christian history from which we may learn things for our own assistance as we try to tread the paths which they too tried to follow. But it is important not to try to find in their experiences detailed instructions for ourselves. What are helpful are the underlying principles on which they based their successful attempts to do the will of God, and these have to be adopted and applied in the situations of to-day.

There is much of great value to be found if these truths are kept in mind. Christianity is an historical religion: that is a statement which is often repeated, and it is true. But it is also an eternal religion in the sense of being timeless with God. History for Christians is not something which happened in the past only; it is the outbreak into the here and now of the living power of God through his Word active in the lives of men. What St Augustine experienced 1,600 years ago, for example, is not merely a nice tale of the past, it is part of the ever-living and ever-present life and memory of the Church. For in the Church life and memory are the same, both part of the living love of God.

So, of course, with Jesus Christ. His life is not just something which took place 2,000 years ago in Palestine. It is the ever-living, ever-revealing expression of the eternal present truth of God which reaches out to us now as it did then. It is one example, the supreme example and the unique example, of the outbreak of God into this world of sin to bring it back to him. And because of that a series of outbreaks of a lesser kind have continually occurred before and since and are occurring at this very minute. This is the spiritual life—the life of God making itself manifest in the world in the everyday lives of men.

Thus the spiritual life in its widest sense embraces every aspect of life on this earth, physical, mental, and "spiritual" in its narrower sense. The word will have to be used in this narrow sense in discussing the life of prayer and similar activities. But the wider meaning should not be forgotten, for the life of prayer must find its place in the wider spiritual life.

As regards the traditional division of the nature of man into body, mind, and spirit, it must be recognized that this is an artificial division only convenient for certain limited uses. In this division body and mind fall into one division and spirit into the other. In other words body and mind are two aspects of the machinery with which the personality of man works, whereas spirit is the essence of the personality itself. Mind may indeed prove to be merely another aspect of body, in the sense that the mental processes are connected with the brain and can only be conducted with the brain. The power of reasoning, however, belongs to the personality as such, and it is the mind which provides the instrument of applying it, just as the choice of doing physical acts belongs to the personality as such and the body provides the instrumental means for achieving its purpose.

These distinctions are of some importance since there is often some confusion between the words mind, psyche, soul, and spirit. Here "soul" and "spirit" will be used interchangeably to refer to the essential personal man as distinct from the instruments of mind (psyche) and body which the personality has been given to express itself.

The tradition of the Bible is to stress the unity of man, of body and spirit, and not to make the distinctions which were common to Greek philosophy. The idea of the immortality of the soul comes from Greek sources, whereas the biblical emphasis is mainly on the resurrection of the body, that is the redeeming of the whole man. The New Testament idea of the soul "assumes the unity of human nature in its material and immaterial elements, which it does not so clearly distinguish as we are inclined to do;

it emphasizes the worth of human personality, especially by the appeal to its eternal destiny; and it finds the realization of this worth in the moral values of a society constituted through the corporate and individual surrender of personality to the Spirit of God (or Christ)".[1]

The various questions which arose about the nature of the soul and its relation to God had not come to the point of discussion in New Testament times but came later to attract much attention in the Church. The close relation of soul to body has been an element in Christianity which has clashed with Greek traditions. The belief that both are necessary for the human personality does not mean that there is any surrender of the belief that the soul survives after death.

> The view of the body as an integral factor, though not, in its present form, a permanent element, in the slowly-evolved self of personality, would agree with the whole evolutionary history of the world, in which human personality offers the highest values attained, and gathers up so many factors of the process. Philosophically this implies the spiritualization of the body, as against the materialization of the soul; but both elements, body and soul, are real, and form a unity for Christian anthropology and ethics.[2]

Soul and body, therefore, when used to delineate the whole of man's nature are not to be thought to exclude mind, but to include it in the overall part of man which is at the service of the soul. So that in considering the spiritual life we see that mind and body form the instruments, with which each man has been endowed, to be put at the service of his soul or personality, according to his own choice and decision. It is not to be taken that the thoughts of the mind cannot be governed by spiritual control, just the contrary: it is through the mind that the soul is able to find and keep the truth which God has provided for its guidance and fulfilment.

In a recent book[3] the then Professor of Modern History at Cambridge University, Dom David Knowles, begins by discussing the nature of mystical theology. He does not give a very clear

---

[1] *Encyclopaedia of Religion and Ethics.* Art. on "Soul".
[2] Op. cit.   [3] *The English Mystical Tradition.*

picture, and although much of what he says is illuminating and helpful, his conclusions are not altogether convincing. He begins by remarking that there are three kinds of knowledge—natural theology, revealed theology, and mystical theology. This is what he writes:

> Beyond these kinds of knowledge [natural and revealed truths] there is a third by which God and the truths of Christianity can not only be believed and acted upon, but can in varying degrees be directly known and experienced. Such at least is the traditional teaching of the Church, reinforced by the express declarations of theologians and saintly Christians throughout the centuries from the days of the apostles to our own time. This knowledge, this experience, which is never entirely separable from an equally immediate and experimental union with God by love, has three main characteristics. It is recognized as something utterly different from and more real and adequate than all his previous knowledge and love of God. It is experienced as something at once immanent and received, something moving and filling the powers of the mind and soul. It is felt as taking place at a deeper level of the personality and soul than that on which the normal processes of thought and will take place, and the mystic is aware, both in himself and in others, of the soul, its qualities and of the divine presence and action within it, as something wholly distinct from the reasoning mind with its powers. Finally, this experience is wholly incommunicable, save as a bare statement, and in this respect all the utterances of the mystics are entirely inadequate as representations of the mystical experience, but it brings absolute certainty to the mind of the recipient. This is the traditional mystical theology, the mystical knowledge of God, in its purest form.[1]

We shall have something to say later upon the subject, but it is well now to reflect on what Fr Knowles says. First we may say that what he describes is indeed mystical experience, but that his views do not carry conviction when he limits mystical life to those who fall within this particular category of definition. The main exception which we must take is to the subjective test which he has established, namely that mystical experience is *only* what is "recognized by the person concerned as something utterly

[1] Op. cit., p. 2.

different"; that "it is felt as taking place at a deeper level". It seems to rule out what Christian life in fact demonstrates, that there are many Christians who have this experience without being able to explain it to themselves, and without having thoughts about it which are as coherent as those which Fr Knowles's description requires. It is rather like saying that only those who perform with a world famous orchestra are truly musical, when what we see there is merely a highly articulate and well developed musical experience and talent, which is real in the lives of many deeply musical people who would be totally incapable of talking about the depth of experiences which they receive through the beauty of music in many forms.

We may learn from the articulate writers about mysticism, what is its nature, how it can develop in certain personalities, and the kind of experiences which they have, even though the incommunicability of its inner nature remains. But at the same time we must recognize the truth of the statement made by William Temple that "religious experience is the special way in which the whole of life is experienced by the 'religious' man".[1] This quotation perhaps goes too far in the generalizing direction, but the truth lies between the two. It is not satisfactory to represent the mystical life as a specialized section of the Christian life as a whole, and attempts to do so can only be successful at the expense of an adequate doctrine of God's work in the Christian soul.

There is a strong tradition which divides the prayer life into two halves: the first half up to and including the prayer of simple regard is the province of ascetical theology, and the second half is that of mystical theology. But the whole assumption that the particular experiences of the mystics are different in kind from those of ordinary Christians needs to be questioned. Even more unsatisfactory is the theory that the first half is something which can be more or less guaranteed to all Christians who work hard enough at it, but that the rest is the gift of God which cannot be earned in this way. Such a distinction is unacceptable for it makes an arbitrary division in the Christian life binding upon God—so

[1] *Christus Veritas.* Quoted by Martin Thornton, *Pastoral Theology: A Reorientation*, p. 147.

to speak. The whole of the Christian life is dependent upon God's grace and upon man's efforts: looked at in one light, there is nothing that can be done by man without the grace and direct assistance of God; looked at in another light, it is only when man responds to the love of God that God enters into his life and draws man closer and closer to himself. Both are different aspects of the same truth of the love of God, which alone is strong enough to bring men along the right path, and which does in fact do so, yet is strong enough too not to insist upon doing so to the overthrowing of the freedom of man's will which by God's gift in creation is what makes him a man.

All Christians, therefore, can and must aspire to the mystical life, but they cannot aspire to any particular mystical experiences: this is where the vital distinction comes. God gives to each man a distinctive personality with its own possibilities and limitations. Not everyone can be a great composer (if we may use a musical illustration again), but all may and should develop their musical capabilities to their utmost possibility and, in doing so, fulfil the plan of God in that way. The music of heaven in the spiritual life is not confined to selected people, there are no persons who are totally unmusical spiritually. Each has his own gift: he may be able to sing or to play an instrument or to conduct an orchestra or to be inspired by the great music of the spirit which reaches his ears. The mystics are those who are specially gifted in some particular aspect of the spiritual life, to which the notions of higher and lower do not apply. Of course to develop their potentialities is higher than to leave them dormant. But their development is different from and not necessarily higher than another form of the spiritual life which they may not know, but which is the mainspring of another personality. The solo pianist in a piano concerto is not higher than the anonymous second violinist: he is different, and both enjoy and fulfil each other's musical life. So it is with the things of the spirit.

It is, however, of particular value to hear from those who have specialized on certain parts of the spiritual life what general principles they have learned in doing so, for it is by understanding them that all Christians can find what are the basic truths about life with and in God which apply to all, whether they are called to one specialized vocation or to another. All learn from them just as the mystics learn from one another, or one musician learns from another, even though their musical activities may be very diverse.

Ascetical theology and mystical theology are not, therefore, two different disciplines, but the same one under different aspects. Both deal with the principles which underlie the development of the Christian life for all Christians, who without exception are called by God to live their lives in him in union with Christ, and to follow the path of prayer, and to receive in whatever way suits them best the deeper understanding and knowledge of God which comes only through lives of prayer and obedience to his will.

3

The Will

Kierkegaard entitled one of his books *Purity of heart is to will one thing*, thus stating a profound truth before the reader opened the covers. "Will" is a term which is constantly used in speaking or writing about the Christian life. It comes in the basic Christian prayer, "Thy will be done", and it is part of the vocabulary of writers on the spiritual life from the earliest times until the present day. Since it is a key word in much of the discussions of this and allied subjects it is important to spend a short time in considering its meaning.

In modern times some psychologists have tried to get rid of the word on the grounds that its use belongs to a conception of the human personality which is out of date. It has, they think, been used as if it were a separate faculty of the human personality which can be isolated from the rest: but no such faculty exists and its use, therefore, ought to be eschewed.

Such a contention might be acceptable if there were any other word which would do the work of the word "will". But in fact the word and the meaning attached to it are indispensable for the purpose of discussing the spiritual life, or indeed any part of the human personality.

The basic points were considered quite adequately as long ago as 1894 by J. R. Illingworth in his Bampton Lectures entitled, *Personality, Human and Divine*. He strongly emphasized the unity of personality and drew attention to the dangers of speaking of thought, desire, and will as really separable just because they are given different names. "Will" is personality in that aspect in which it comes to a decision to act in some way or other. It is the aspect of personality which gives direction by choice. Other aspects such as desire or thought are not exclusively acts of choice since they may come unbidden into the mind. But the will is the personality in the act of choosing, of self-determination.

This meaning of the word "will" was again pointed out by Dr Austin Farrer in his Gifford Lectures for 1957, *The Freedom of the Will*. In defining free will and the relation of willing and doing he writes:

> "Will" is action itself, in the full and personal sense of the verb to "act". But if so, why do we bother to have two words, "act" and "will", and why, when they are set side by side, do we resist the suggestion that they are synonymous? Because they denote the single fact under different aspects: "act" emphasising what I perform, and "will" my choice, energy or interest in the performance of it. We call nothing an exercise of will which does not constitute an act, though the act may be invisible and internal, say the registration of a decision for my guidance to-morrow.[1]

We are not here concerned to deal with all the niceties of language or with the philosophical problems involved. It is enough to establish the respectability and permissibility of using the concept of "will" in connection with the human personality. It is a necessary concept, though the warnings against isolating it from the rest of the personality must be remembered.

Objections to the use of the word "will" have perhaps been most strongly focused on its use as a "faculty" of human nature. In all these matters the exact use of words is difficult and confusing, for there is no complete agreement as to what each word ought properly to convey. K. E. Kirk makes this point:

> In one way or another the four virtues [Cardinal virtues] are always found referred to the three main elements in consciousness—the intellect, the appetites, and the "active" principle, or will. Modern psychology has done much to define the various terms employed to designate these three elements and to analyse afresh the manner in which they co-operate. It deprecates the application to them of any such name as "faculties" implying the possibility of their separate and independent existences; for it recognises that consciousness is an indivisible unit whose "parts" are no more than

[1] Op. cit., p. 110.

logical abstractions. At the same time it reaffirms the psychology of less scientific days by recognising the same three "regions" or factors as operative in every conscious action: the cognitive, the appetitive and the conative—intellect, desire, and will or purpose.[1]

In a footnote to this passage Kirk points out that there may be an ambiguity in the use of the word "will", but that to any person who admits the reality of free will it must mean the formed purpose which governs acts and is the final motive in reasoned action. These passages would seem to provide enough demonstration that the use of the concept of the will is still legitimate, and indeed that it is necessary in order to refer to the inmost and most important act of the personality.

In a strictly psychological study of the mind the verb "to will" is preferred to the noun. "To will" is to choose, or to intend, or to overcome obstruction.[2] This is another way of trying to safeguard the relation of the act of will to the other elements in the personality. But always to use the verb would make discussion hopelessly clumsy. It would prevent a simple phrase such as a "strong will" and require a circumlocution such as "the acquired habit of putting into practice the choices he had made".

As Kirk suggests in the quotation already given, there was a psychology of less scientific days. This is not always recognized, and many people are under the impression that psychology is a new study. Quite the contrary is the case: it is probably as old as any other study in the world. The difference between earlier and modern methods is in the attempt to categorize the results and to phrase them in a new language of its own.

Psychology is an observed science, based on the careful and practical observations of human nature. The treatment of psychological conditions can only come from experience in observing and dealing with the different conditions of personal life as they present themselves in their infinite variety. This is exactly what the teachers of the spiritual life and the directors of Christian people have been doing for centuries past. The fact

[1] *Some Principles of Moral Theology*, p. 38.
[2] R. S. Woodworth and D. G. Marquis, *Psychology. A study of mental life*, p. 368.

that they do not use the same technical terms as have been adopted in the twentieth century should not blind us to the fact that they work in a field closely allied to that of the modern psychiatrists. Methods of treatment or spiritual exercises which have been proved in practice over long periods of time stand justified by their results, just as much as those which have been learnt recently.

The directors of the spiritual life are dealing with specific aspects of the human personality, distinct from that of the ordinary psychologist, though overlapping in important respects. The object of spiritual direction is the encouragement of the growth of the Christian personality in the ways of God. In pursuing this aim teachers have studied the obstacles which intrude themselves and the best ways of overcoming them. It is true, of course, that some of the explanations which in earlier times were given for observed phenomena have now been discarded. But the scepticism of some modern commentators has gone too far in trying to discount the spiritual powers which were thought to be active in men's lives, a scepticism sometimes adopted because to the modern specialist in psychology the presence of such spiritual powers introduces an unknown factor into his calculations which would make them much more difficult and less certain.

It is, therefore, reasonable to continue to use time-honoured words as "will" in the spiritual life, always bearing in mind that the terms are abstractions from the whole personality and for the most part cannot be more than approximations to what is meant. But they remain the necessary tools for the fruitful consideration of this most important part of human life.

We now need to examine in more detail the part of the will in the Christian life in all its aspects, and especially in Christian prayer, for it plays the paramount rôle in the whole of the Christian life.

Our first observations should clearly come from the New Testament, and if this is examined dispassionately there can be no doubt that it is the attitude of the will which is shown to be the decisive part of a man's religion. The point is not discussed there in exactly the same terms as came to be used later, but if the contents of the New Testament are analysed it is evidently the will which is regarded as all important. To make this point clearer we must note that the will is exercised in the choice which a person makes as regards his actions. What a man feels and what he thinks are only partly at his command, and, although it may be admitted that his freedom of action may be limited to some extent by feelings and thought, yet there always remains the freedom of choice which is the particular function of the will. We can, therefore, equate our conception of the will with the choices men make in their actions.

Jesus frequently teaches the importance of obedience. He does so very clearly in St John's Gospel where the teaching which he is giving about love refers not to the emotions of love but to the act of the will which chooses to obey. "If ye keep my commandments, ye shall abide in my love; even as I have kept my Father's commandments, and abide in his love. . . . Greater love hath no man than this, that a man lay down his life for his friends. Ye are my friends, if ye do whatsoever I command you." (John 15. 10, 13f.) It is difficult to imagine anything plainer than this. Moreover, the whole life of Jesus is the working out of this great truth in history. The crucifixion is the full expression of his love because he obeyed God and suffered. His feelings sometimes pressed him in another direction, as we can learn from looking at the agony in the Garden of Gethsemane, but this did not affect the love which he showed in perfect obedience.

So it is with the other teaching of our Lord. Again and again he points out that it is by our actions that our attitude to God is shown, that is, by our wills which alone can issue in right action and which cannot be right without issuing in action. So the parables of the good Samaritan, Dives and Lazarus, the sheep and the goats, the prodigal son, and many others all show that love is only discovered through the will which, whatever the feelings may be, acts in obedience to that love. Thus we may legitimately infer that the feelings of the Samaritan towards the injured Jew were not necessarily warm. Indeed it is obvious that the Samaritan has been chosen for the example in the parable just because feelings between Samaritans and Jews were as bad as could be.

Yet it was the man who was least inclined by his feelings to show love, who did in fact give the example of love by helping the injured Jew. And the conclusion of the parable is not that the lawyer should feel loving but should go and do likewise, for it is in the doing that the love consists, and in the doing alone that the love is shown, and the doing is the immediate result of the will making a choice.

This truth is of immense importance in the Christian life, and is often misunderstood by many people who are earnest Christians. The modern age has largely lost the sense of duty, and, indeed, to do a thing from duty is often spoken of as though it were something rather low. But the truth is that the sense of duty is the highest sense of which man is capable, for it is the sense of what is owing to God in obedience, and shows itself in the decisions of the will to walk his path. It is, of course, agreeable if the path of duty is a pleasant one, but it is not necessarily to be expected, and is often quite the contrary. Thorns, passion, and suffering are the hallmarks of the life of Christ whose life is pre-eminently a life of duty, wholly fulfilled. In the past it has sometimes been thought that if duty was unpleasant, that must make it right. This is a *non sequitur*, and if God allows our duty to be pleasant, that is a cause of great thankfulness. But there should be no doubt that duty, and duty alone, is the Christian call to all who claim that name.

It is evident to any thinking person that there is almost nothing worth while in this world which can be achieved without con-centrated effort and application, irrespective of temporary feelings of distaste. If men examine their own lives they will find that all the most important things in life have to be conducted whether they feel like it or not, for otherwise their lives would fall to pieces. It would not be thought very satisfactory for a man to say that he would support his family only when he felt like it, and those who undertake other less essential work find the same truth. So the will is seen to be the key to the creative and con-structive life.

The effect of this news on some people will be to depress them, but it should do just the opposite. For it is good news, and is at the heart of the Gospel. Were the feelings which are not under our control to be the decisive element in religion it would put us at the beck and call of all kinds of forces, evil as well as good, and we should be like a small boat without a tiller driven backwards and forwards in a gale. Were our minds to be the decisive part of the personality, Christianity would become a religion open only to those who had reached a certain grade of intellectual ability. There have been a number of heresies (usually called Gnostic) which have tried to make Christianity into this kind of religion, something for those who had a special knowledge of it. But because the will is the key, the hope of the Christian religion is within the capabilities of every one of us, rich or poor, simple or sophisticated, clever or stupid, for it is a matter of character and not of skill or temperament.

A warning mentioned elsewhere may again be repeated here. When we speak of the will we do not envisage it as the controlling feature of the personality by any efforts of its own, we merely mark it out as the key point in the life of the person, and the point to which attention must be mainly given. The activities of the will form a subject, which must be considered separately from the fact of the will's central position in the Christian life. When the will has been revealed in its proper rôle, its use in the approach to God can be considered in its true proportion.

The central importance of the will provides the context in which we can see the true nature of sin, and why it is so important. Sin consists in the fact that the will is directed away from God towards some end which is opposed to the will of God. That is why in the Greek the word for repentance means change of mind from another outlook to that which God desires us to have. It is the turning away from God which makes it impossible for a person to partake of God's love, because this turning away is the deliberate rejection of it. Dom Augustine Morris writes:

The conclusion is inescapable: unless the sinner be separated from his sin, he will perish with it. This is an inexorable law, and is a necessary consequence of the very nature of sin as being an offence against the love of God. If by sin the will is set in opposition to God, then it is incapable of receiving the love of God. It is not that the

24

love of God is any less, but that the sinner's will has stubbornly taken up a position opposed to that of love. The light is not lessened by the fact that I will not look upon it. "This is the judgement, that the light is come into the world, and men loved the darkness rather than the light; for their works were evil." (John 3. 19.)[1]

To face the effects of turning away from God should not lead to despair, and the words just quoted do not refer to individual acts of sin, but to the deliberate choice of the will in rejecting God. All fall into sins until the time that God makes them perfect, but his infinite love reaches out to them in their sins and brings them back to him, if they turn towards him in repentance.

So in prayer it is the will to pray that is all important, whatever may seem to be the difficulties and obstacles which appear when effort to pray is actually taking place.

> But in all these things, it is the will to pray that is the essence of prayer, and the desire to find God and to see Him and to love Him is the one thing that matters. If you have desired to know Him and love Him you have already done what was expected of you, and it is much better to desire God without being able to think clearly of Him, than to have marvellous thoughts about Him without desiring to enter into union with His will.[2]

"The aim and object of all spiritual life is the union of the will with the holy will of God", wrote St John of the Cross.[3] This is the note which echoes and re-echoes through the whole world of spiritual writing, and all discussions about the spiritual life are centred around the question of how to make this principle a reality in the actual lives of Christians. But until the importance of the will in the Christian's personal life is understood, it is impossible to go further in understanding its rôle in the life of prayer. Moreover, the prayer life appears too difficult and far removed from the ordinary Christian until this point is appreciated.

Drexelius in his work *The Heliotropium* had as his sub-title the "Conformity of the human will to the divine". In it he showed the same awareness as other writers that it is here that the centre

---

[1] *Straight Course to God*, p. 27.
[2] Thomas Merton, *Seeds of Contemplation*, p. 84.
[3] *Dark Night of the Soul*, pt. 2, ch. 16, sec. 10.

of the matter is to be found, the disposition of the human will and its submission to God. St Francis de Sales showed the same attitude when he wrote: "Even so is our heart conformed to God's, when by holy benevolence we throw all our affections into the hands of the divine will, to be turned and directed as he chooses, to be moulded and formed to its good liking."[1] This is done by an act of the will, which, throughout the whole gamut of the Christian and spiritual life from the earliest beginnings to the most advanced union with God, is seen to be the key to all growth and love.

An examination of the main qualities which are needed for the Christian life strengthens the convictions which we have just stated. It is found when they are analysed in their essence that it is the will to which they owe their reality. We have already touched on this in dealing with love and have seen that in our Lord's teaching the essence of love is in the will, in what a man is prepared to do for the one who is loved. Love is shown in obedience, in duty, in action, not in indulging the feelings or inclinations.

The same truth is found in an examination of the virtue of patience, which is so important in the New Testament and in the spiritual life. The word *hupomone* means more accurately "patient endurance", for example in Luke 8.15, and it depends on the will. "It is a lively outgoing power of faith, an active energy rather than a passive resignation."[2] It is in fact the expression of the will.

Faith is a concept which also finds itself rooted in the will. This is not the place to try to examine all its richness, nor the many false ideas which are current in the world about what Christians mean when they speak of "faith". Faith includes many aspects, of which belief in certain events is not the only nor even the most important side. The popular notion that faith means believing in something which ordinary people think to be unreasonable is a sign of how far its true meaning has been obscured, and how far Christians have failed to exhibit its depth in their presentation of the Gospel to others. Faith in its basic meaning is trust in a person, in God and in Christ. Such trust is

[1] *Treatise on the Love of God*, bk. viii, ch. 2.
[2] R. Gregor Smith, *A Theological Word Book of the Bible*, p. 165.

not dependent on the feelings but on the will. Dean Inge truly wrote, "Faith begins with an experiment and ends with an experience". And the experiment is a decision of the will: in its essence it is the choice between God and his substitutes, when a man says, "I will choose God and trust my life to him".

Faith itself and acts of faith may, of course, be accompanied by highly emotional experiences, especially in the moment of conversion which some people experience. But what distinguishes that moment from all other moments is the fact, not that there was an experience, but that there was a decision. The emotions caused the will to act, and it was in that act that faith was born.

A corollary is the important fact that faith in God can exist strongly at the same time as doubts about certain particular events in Christian history or in popular interpretation of the Christian religion. Doubt is a form of intellectual questioning which is a natural expression of the powers of the reason, but it differs only in degree from that proper agnosticism which all Christians must have about God. There is always a vast area of truth about God which, when questions are asked, must always produce the answer "I don't know". As Dr Mascall says:

The bald and dogmatic phrases of *Quicunque vult* [the Athanasian Creed] may disappoint those who look for an explanation, but when we are dealing with the mysteries of the inner being of God, explanation is not what we need. Indeed, any explanation that professed to be adequate would *ipso facto* condemn itself, for among the few certain things in life we may surely reckon this—that we finite creatures cannot hope to explain the mysteries of God.[1]

Faith, then, is not primarily a mental exercise, but a man committing himself by an act of will to the providence of God, and determining to base his life on that act. This is the teaching of the Old and New Testaments: "The faith to which Jesus summons men is confident conviction that God, through His Messiah, was able to do what he had promised through the prophets. It is decisive response to the proffered resources of God, directly present now in the flesh of His Son."[2]

[1] *Death or Dogma?* p. 37.
[2] W. A. Whitehouse, *A Theological Word Book of the Bible*, p. 76.

It is because faith and love are inextricably bound up together in the Christian message that the understanding of the part which the will must play is so important. The act of faith is in itself an act of love because it is the free giving of the will to God in spite of uncertainties and doubts which may intellectually be present. If Christianity were merely a matter of intellectual certainty it would partake of the nature of a mathematical problem and would be evacuated of its possibilities of love, for there is something in love which requires a man to commit himself to the partly unknown. This is true of the forms of human love which we know on earth, and it is even more evident in the love of God. This feature of love is bound up with the fact that it is a relationship between persons and cannot therefore be reduced to mere logical analysis or calculation.

Another analogy may be used. Love cannot exist where there is no freedom to withhold love. It is impossible to call forth love from a man by merely proving by demonstration that another person loves him. This is partly because such proof can never be fully convincing unless there is already some direct experience of the reality of the love in question. Love is called forth only through the free response of one person to the reality of another person's love. Or it can, as with God's love for us, be showered on a person without any reason to justify it from the point of view of the worthiness of the recipient. This side of love is well brought out by Dr Nygren in his work which is discussed elsewhere. True love must be free if the word "love" is not to be emptied of its essential meaning.

Faith, therefore, must also be free in the same sense, and because both are free, they essentially rest on the free choice of the will.

I CORINTHIANS 13

The most complete confirmation of the preceding emphasis that the essence of love resides in the will and in action, rather than in the emotions or mind, is to be found in St Paul's thirteenth chapter of his first letter to the Corinthians, which may be claimed as the classical exposition of the nature of love in the New Testament.

He begins by distinguishing sharply between love and powers of persuasive and stirring speech ("the tongues of men and of angels"). These can be had without love; so also can powers of prophecy, and brilliant intellectual achievement ("understand all mysteries and all knowledge"). Even faith can be had without love and is distinct from it, and last of all the self-sacrifice of martyrdom, which many Christians have thought to be the ultimate height of Christian attainment, can occur without love.

These are sensational statements, and it is only because Christians have become used to the statements of the Bible that they so often fail to feel their cutting edge. The word of God is like a two-edged sword, but very often Christians have somehow managed to defend themselves against its effects by surrounding themselves with thick impenetrable woolly clothing. Almost all of the things mentioned by St Paul in the first three verses of this chapter have at some time or other been lesser gods for Christians, whose profession ought to have made them foreswear anything of the kind.

Unhappily it remains true that the gifts most admired by Christians are still often those which St Paul here characterizes as lesser gifts, so much "lesser" that without love they are nothing or worse than nothing. The priest who is admired is so often the man with the power of winning speech, or of prophecy, or of learning. All are here condemned when they are without love. On the other side the effort of the individual Christian is often aimed at faith by itself, which may become a kind of spiritual self-deception; or at the achievement of a Christian activity by generosity of self-denial. But these too without love are empty.

Having stated these things in a dramatic manner St Paul goes on to describe what love is and what it is not. Love is patient and kind; it rejoices in the right; bears all things, believes all things, hopes all things, endures all things. This is interesting for it comes back to the contrasts which he has just made. In other words he says that faith without love is nothing, but then goes on to say that love has all faith within it (believes all things); that martyrdom without love is useless, but that love includes martyrdom (endures all things). Here we find the key to the whole chapter, and indeed to the whole of the Christian life. Love is what gives meaning to life from start to finish. Without it there is no relationship to God, but only a loyalty to smaller things which are therefore idols standing in the place where they should not.

Finally St Paul tells his readers that love never ends—it is eternal, but all the other things will pass away. It is eternal, of course, because it is a sharing in the life of God who is love. But this sharing does not depend on human achievements, even though these may in some cases be found in association with it. Nor does it depend on human feelings or apparent gifts. Love is something which is shown in its actions and attitudes towards others—it is patient and kind. It is neither jealous nor boastful, arrogant nor rude, irritable nor resentful. So the basic meaning of love is shown to reside in that part of the human personality where attitudes are chosen, not where they are felt.

Faith, hope, and love are stated as three distinct virtues, but St Paul has already shown that both hope and faith are only understood when they are included as part of and ruled by love ("hopeth all things, believeth all things"). Love must rule in the heart, and, if it does so, it will supply the other virtues which are needed for the fullest life in God. And love is that decision by which the person adheres or clings to God by his will, by his free choice, and commits himself completely to doing his will, whatever may be the imperfections of his emotional condition or the temptations with which he has to wrestle in order to do so. Indeed, the love exists so long as the will is directed aright, even when he falls into manifold temptations and errs from the right way, so long as he chooses to return to that way and to follow it patiently and persistently, by rising from his fall and coming back to the way that leads to salvation—submission to the will of God.

FURTHER THOUGHTS ON THE WILL

The centrality of the will remains. Yet as we consider the matter we see that this idea may be misunderstood. We have already suggested that the will is not to be considered as a series of human acts of self-help which lift the soul to God. Such an idea is completely mistaken and spiritually deadly. The importance of the will lies in the fact that it chooses the direction in which the spirit will look. Simone Weil wished to replace this idea by saying that it is really desire which is the basic fact, and this too contains truth. But the desire is something which is closely allied to the will, for the act of looking to God, which is the outcome of desire, is an act of choice, and that springs from the will. So the centrality of the will is not to be thought of as an activist operation, but more as a passive-active waiting upon God and looking to him. It is in short the will to submit to God.

Simone Weil's words put the point thus, though there are some expressions from which one must dissent:

The will is on the level of the natural part of the soul. The right use of the will is a condition of salvation, necessary no doubt but remote, inferior, very subordinate and purely negative. The weeds are pulled up by the muscular effort of the peasant, but only sun and water can make the corn grow. The will cannot produce any good in the soul.

Efforts of the will are only in their right place for carrying out definite obligations. Wherever there is no strict obligation we must follow either our natural inclination or our vocation, that is to say God's command. Actions prompted by our inclination do not involve an effort of will. In our acts of obedience to God we are passive; whatever difficulties we have to surmount, however great our activity may appear to be, there is nothing analagous to muscular effort; there is only waiting, attention, silence, immobility, constant through suffering and joy. The crucifixion of Christ is the model of all acts of obedience.

This kind of passive activity, the highest of all, is perfectly described in the Baghavat-Ghita and in Lao-Tse. Also there is a supernatural union of opposites, a harmony in the Pythagorean sense.

That we have to strive after goodness with an effort of our will is one of the lies invented by the mediocre part of ourselves in its fear of being destroyed. Such an effort does not threaten it in any way, it does not even disturb its comfort—not even when it entails a great deal of fatigue and suffering. For the mediocre part of ourselves is not afraid of fatigue and suffering, it is afraid of being killed. . . .

It is because the will has no power to bring about salvation that the idea of secular morality is an absurdity. What is called morality only depends on the will in what is, so to speak, its most muscular aspect. Religion on the contrary corresponds to desire, and it is desire which saves.[1]

To put the will on the level of the natural part of the soul is an artificiality which can only mislead, for the soul cannot be divided in this way. Desire is just as much on this natural level as the will, but both are transformed by God's influence. Moreover, the will is not confined to definite obligations, but makes the decision or choice of the soul to look towards God. To take the crucifixion of Christ as the model of all acts of obedience is indeed right, but it includes the effort of the Garden of Gethsemane, where the central drama was the act of the will in which Christ submitted his will to the will of God. The difficulty is partly one of words, none of which are wholly adequate to express the kernel of the matter.

On the other hand the warnings which Simone Weil gives against considering religion as a kind of self-lifting by acts of the will are quite correct and necessary. The will's task—helped by God—is to keep our gaze on him. She says: "It is at those moments when we are, as we say, in a bad mood, when we feel incapable of the elevation of soul which befits holy things, it is then that it is most effectual to turn our eyes towards perfect purity. For it is then that evil, or rather mediocrity, comes to the surface of the soul and is in the best position for being burnt by contact with the fire." And what is this turning of our eyes to God if it is not an act of the will in the sense we have adopted?

[1] *Waiting on God*, p. 146.

4

The Mind

It is clearly a prime principle of the Christian religion that the mind of man has been given him by God to be used, and that no form of religion which abrogates the powers of human reason can be fully Christian. On the other hand the mind is an instrument for something else; it is not the centre of the Christian character. This has been already seen to be the will. Nevertheless, the reason is one faculty which distinguishes man from the rest of the animal creation, and must not be underestimated.

St Thomas Aquinas wrote: "The intellect is a power of the soul, and not the very essence of the soul. . . . in God alone is His intellect His essence: while in other intellectual creatures, the intellect is a power."[1] He goes on to discuss whether the intellect is greater than the will or vice versa, and concludes that each may be higher than the other according to the point of approach which is chosen, but that the will is the means by which the decision of choice is taken.

There has been a tendency in some writers to underestimate the importance of the mind in prayer, but this has come from a misunderstanding of the rôle which it must play. The act of prayer is not primarily an intellectual activity, but nevertheless the intellect can play an important and constructive part in it. Moreover, prayer cannot exist without some help from the intellect, for the very concept of prayer must first be present to the mind before the person can take part in it, and this concept is an intellectual apprehension. In other words no man can start to pray unless he has some idea about what prayer is and what is its object.

[1] I. 3rd number. Q.LXXIX. Art. i.

On the other hand prayer, being basically an act of the will, cannot be identified with mental activity, even though such activity may be of considerable help to it. St Thomas à Kempis puts the point forcibly in his first chapter of *The Imitation of Christ*:

> What will it avail thee to dispute profoundly of the Trinity, if thou be void of humility, and art thereby displeasing to the Trinity?
>
> Surely high words do not make a man holy and just; but a virtuous life maketh him dear to God.
>
> I had rather feel compunction, than understand the definition thereof.
>
> If thou didst know the whole Bible by heart, and the sayings of all the philosphers, what would all that profit thee without the love of God and without grace?

In an age when the power of the human intellect, at any rate in its scientific application, is often thought to be the key to everything good in life, it is a wholesome corrective to learn that in Christian teaching the deepest things are beyond the reach of the intellect alone.

On the other hand the entirely negative approach, typified by the writings of the so-called Dionysius the Areopagite, may go beyond the true Christian tradition and lead to the exclusion of the intellect in a way which impoverishes the Gospel, both in its proclamation and in its life in the individual soul. "Leave behind", he wrote, "the senses and the operations of the intellect, and all things sensible and intellectual, and all things in the world of being and non-being, that thou mayest arise by Unknowing towards the union, so far as it is attainable, with Him who transcends all being, and all knowledge."[1]

This approach has had a strong influence in Christian mysticism, a simple example being seen in the well-known fourteenth-century work whose very title emphasizes the point—*The Cloud of Unknowing*. In discussing the teaching of the Gospel incident of Martha and Mary the unidentified writer distinguishes the two good but lesser activities of bodily works of mercy and meditation on the truths of the Christian religion from the

---

[1] *The Mystical Theology*, ch. 1.

highest part which is prayer beyond the powers of thought. "The third part of these two lives hangeth in this dark cloud of unknowing, with many a privy love pressed to God by Himself."[1]

These writers are stating an important truth, but it has to be seen in its right perspective if it is to be understood. They are emphasizing the impossibility of the mind fully understanding God. It is the truth expressed in the Athanasian Creed—that God is incomprehensible, too great to be measured and comprehended by the finite minds of his creatures. But this does not take away from the right use of the mind, when it is exercised in proportion to the other parts of the personality.

The sense of the incomprehensibility of God is strongly stressed in many Eastern Orthodox writers, who particularly value what is known as the apophatic method of writing of God, whereby he is described only in negatives. The reason for this is simple: every positive human attribute is tainted by the inadequate associations which are tied to it in human life, and therefore cannot properly or exactly be applied to God who is far above all such attributes. Therefore God is only to be described by saying what he is not.

For ordinary preaching or exposition of the Gospel this approach is not suitable. Moreover it does not accord with the methods of teaching of our Lord himself, who must be the model for any who claim to be speaking with his authentic voice. Yet it is clear that the importance of intellectual attainment was not a matter of first importance in our Lord's outlook, and his attitude to the Scribes suggests that he was acutely aware of its dangers. However, in more advanced theological discussion the truths which the apophatic method safeguards are of great importance.

The Eastern Orthodox approach may be summed up in the words of Vladimir Lossky:

All that we have said about apophaticism may be summed up in a few words. Negative theology is not merely a theory of ecstasy. It is an expression of that fundamental attitude which transforms the whole of theology into a contemplation of the mysteries of revelation. It is not a branch of theology, a chapter, or an inevitable

[1] Op. cit., ch. 21.

introduction on the incomprehensibility of God from which one passes unruffled to a doctrinal exposition in the usual terminology of human reason and philosophy in general. Apophaticism teaches us to see above all a negative meaning in the dogmas of the Church: it forbids us to follow natural ways of thought and to form concepts which would usurp the place of spiritual realities. For Christianity is not a philosophical school for speculating about abstract concepts, but is essentially a communion with the living God.[1]

What the writer is doing here is to warn us against putting the idols of our own cleverness or imagination in the place in our lives which only God should occupy. He stresses the importance of union with God, as all the true teachers do: it is deification and not knowledge that really matters. This is a warning which must constantly be heeded, and which is often necessary. But it can be taken too far if it is thought to inhibit the use of the mind within the limits which have been noted. The attempt to use the apophatic approach has certain self-contradictory elements in it. It uses the concepts which it is busy condemning. It is difficult to see how one can properly speak of "contemplating" something which is entirely negative. What must be understood is that there is a threshold beyond which the mind cannot step because there is darkness, a darkness which is experienced by those who grow in the life of prayer, a darkness which is caused by light greater than we can bear.

St John of the Cross points out the same truth when he says, "All that the imagination can imagine and the reason conceive and understand in this life is not, and cannot be, a proximate means of union with God."[2] And again in the *Ascent of Mount Carmel*:

For these reasons, therefore, the eyes of the soul must be continually turned aside from these visible and distinctly intelligible things, communicated through the sense, which form neither the foundation nor the security of faith, and be fixed on the invisible, not on the things of sense but on those of the Spirit which are not cognisable by

[1] *Mystical Theology of The Eastern Church*, p. 42.
[2] Quoted by Aldous Huxley, *The Perennial Philosophy*, p. 149.

sense; for it is this that lifts up the soul to union in faith which is the proper medium.[1]

There are, therefore, two stages in the interpretation of the place of the mind favoured by spiritual teachers. In the first stage the intellect is useful as an instrument for leading the spirit to the right approach to God, and it can do much to kindle the flame of the will to follow the path of Christian growth. But it must never become an idol and it must be clearly recognized that at a certain point there is no more that the intellect can do. St Teresa puts it like this:

> Let them be very careful when God gives them these sentiments [love, praise, etc.] not to set them aside in order to finish their accustomed meditation . . . it is not so essential to *think* much as to *love* much. . . . Love does not consist in great sweetness of devotion, but in a fervent determination to strive to please God in all things, in avoiding, so far as possible, all that would offend him, and in praying for the increase of the glory and honour of His Son and for the growth of the Catholic Church . . . do not imagine that it consists in never thinking of anything but God, and that if your thoughts wander a little all is lost.[2]

This brings us to the subject of meditation as understood in the life of prayer. "Meditation" is a general word covering all kinds of thought about spiritual subjects, and it may be applied also to formal schemes of prayer for thinking about scenes from the Bible or other matters which can help towards a better appreciation of the truths of the Christian Faith, with the consequent strengthening of the will and the promotion of sentiments which can aid it in making right decisions.

In some Christian circles meditation has sometimes come to fill the whole place which should be devoted to prayer: prayer has been thought of as consisting of meditation and nothing else. This is a damaging error and can have serious results in the Christian life. The encouragement of formal methods of meditation in England during the last half of the nineteenth and first half of the twentieth century undoubtedly led many to a deeper sense of

[1] Op. cit., bk. ii, ch. 16.
[2] *Interior Castle*, 4th Mansions, ch. 1, para. 7.

their religion, but for some it had the effect of stultifying their life of prayer because they thought that the essence of prayer lay in the form of meditation which they had been taught to practise. Many spiritual persons never heard of other ways of growing in the life of prayer, to which some of them were being called by God.

"Meditation" is "thinking", whether according to some well tried method like the Ignatian, or an informal consideration of some aspect of religion. Its part in the prayer life is to deepen the appreciation of truth and to arouse the will to submit itself to God, perhaps in the form of particular resolutions, but often in other ways. It is not an end in itself, but an instrument for help in the spiritual life. If it is allowed to bulk too large it becomes an obstacle instead of a support. For most people some form of meditation is required at some stage in their prayer life, but it should not become fixed. There are some who will make a meditation in an informal way at a time different from that of their prayer. There are others, especially among the clergy, who spend a great deal of their time thinking about the truths of their Faith and who do not need to fill their time of prayer with meditation, since they have a permanent background of meditation on which to build.

Dom John Chapman points out these facts in his *Spiritual Letters*. When meditation becomes out-dated for any particular person it is sometimes because God is calling him to another form of prayer. He writes:

> The reason why Meditation is impossible is that, when one takes to prayer, the intellect is occupied in doing something else; viz. contemplating. But this Contemplation is so obscure that it is unperceived. It is subconscious like the circulation of the blood, but quite as real. It is deep down at the root of the intellect, and, in unimaginative and unemotional people, has absolutely *no effect* on the imagination and emotions.[1]

This explanation of what happens may appeal to some and not to others. But whatever the correct explanation may be, there is no

[1] *Letter 42.*

doubt about the fact, noted again and again by spiritual directors, that there often comes a time when formal meditations are not only unnecessary but may be an actual hindrance.

The use of the mind in prayer, therefore, is limited in two ways. There is, as we have seen, a boundary beyond which it can no longer usefully formulate intellectual concepts because it has come to the edge of the darkness of God who is greater than our minds. Secondly, in practice there comes a point where the constant activity of the intellect may distract a person from the attention to God which he ought to be giving in other ways. But neither of these limitations in the least takes away from the supreme importance of the intellect within its own dominions as the indispensable instrument for certain purposes within the Christian life.

There can never be any cessation of thinking in the Christian life for it is necessary in the simplest attempt to convey the Gospel from one person to another. It is to be the constant background of the life of every Christian person, but it should not be imported into the acts of prayer in which the practice of the presence of God is carried on, once it has served its purpose there. Nor is it to be exalted as a god to which every other faculty must bow, for the deeper mysteries of the divine work are mediated to man through the spirit.

5

Feelings

The word "feeling" is used to cover a multitude of different experiences, and consequently it often leads to confusion. Modern psychology and certain modern forms of pastoral counselling have so stressed the importance of the feelings that some members of the uninstructed public have been led to think that they are more important than is really the case, or perhaps it would be more accurate to say that they believe their feelings to be of more permanent value than a properly balanced view would allow.

Feelings or emotions in the spiritual life are often mistaken for spiritual achievement—a serious misunderstanding of its true quality—and it is therefore important to try to understand their place. Feeling may be described as "a general term for the affective aspect of experience, i.e. the experience of pleasure and its opposite, interest and the like, usually inclusive of emotional experience; used popularly in an indefinite sense for any experience".[1] This gives a good starting point for defining "feeling" when used of the spiritual life, if the loose popular and indefinite sense mentioned at the end of the quotation is excluded.

If "feeling" is used for any experience, the word becomes so indefinite as to be of little use. In this book the word "feelings" refers to the affective aspects of the spiritual life, especially in the activity of prayer, to the immediate aspects of pleasure or pain experienced in the life of prayer, but excludes the deeper experiences which often exist at the same time as such feelings and are quite different from them. For example it is quite possible for a Christian

[1] James Drever, *A Dictionary of Psychology*, p. 93.

40

to experience total barrenness on the normal plane of his feelings, or even great trials, and yet at the same time to have in the depth of his spirit the "peace of God which passes all understanding".

It would be misleading to say that the feelings are not important in the spiritual life. They are important throughout life, and indeed the affective aspects of human nature belong to the whole, and should normally be expected to play their part in the life of the whole man in whatever particular activity he is engaged. Moreover the right treatment of the feelings in normal life is the key to stability, whereas wrong attitudes can, and often do, lead to psychological crises of one kind or another. Modern research stresses the harmful effects which follow the repression of the feelings and emotions, that is, the refusal to accept them for some reason of guilt or fear, and the forcible expulsion of them from the conscious to the unconscious part of the mind.

Terms are not used exactly in the same way by all the experts. But we are not concerned to go deeply into the technical aspect of the problem: it is enough to note that the wrong treatment of the emotions and of natural desires and impulses can have seriously harmful effects on the personality. It would, therefore, be wrong to underestimate the importance of the feelings, and of their right treatment.

In some modern pastoral counselling the feelings come to play a predominant part in the technique of trying to help those who come for counsel. Indeed it appears that the technique of identifying the counsellor with the feelings of the patient sometimes goes so far that he declines to take any independent attitude towards them. The importance of giving the patient the conviction that the counsellor is in complete sympathy with his point of view sometimes leads to a suggestion by implication that there are no ultimate standards to apply to his problem.

This kind of approach, together with the stress put upon the emotions by certain psychological schools, has led many people to think that the emotions are the decisive thing in life, and that this is the "right" way of looking at them. But here, as in all other matters, it is important to keep a balance so that each part of the human personality may fulfil its purpose in proper relation to the others.

The general public and those dealing with personal problems may easily be tempted to give an exaggerated importance to the feelings, if in fact most of the attention of analysis is concentrated upon them as if they were the only decisive element. They can become decisive either through a wrong approach to them in the first place, or because a person is so unbalanced as to be at the complete mercy of his feelings, in which case he is in a state of mental illness. In both cases there is a twist which leads to a wrong attitude.

The exaltation of the feelings as a guide to life is much encouraged by the popular presentations of television, radio, and film. The public is bombarded by wrong standards which promote the idea that success consists in finding satisfaction for the emotions and superficial feelings. The gross caricature of the true nature of love which is the bread and butter of popular television, cinema, and radio has done much to inculcate wrong standards in the minds of the people and bears a heavy responsibility for the break-up of married lives, the increase of the divorce rate, and increased marital infidelity. The twentieth century of the West has got its popular values hopelessly muddled and inverted.

We are always inclined to think that our own problems are worse than those of earlier generations: sometimes we are right and sometimes wrong. But in the matter of loss of values, there can scarcely be any doubt that the situation is far more chaotic to-day than it was even fifty years ago. There has been a progressive decline in many generally accepted standards, and more and more people find themselves completely confused about values, and in this state of confusion they fall back on the satisfaction of their own temporary and superficial whims as the only guide to action. However wicked men may have been in the Middle Ages, for example, they did all accept Christian standards of morality and value as self-evident guide-posts which they ought to follow, even if they did not. The same might be said of the nineteenth century: but now men either find no guide-posts at all, or so many that they are useless and contradictory.

The tendency to stress the importance of the feelings in Christian life is part of a new understanding of the human personality, but in some cases it has resulted in a rather too subjective approach. Recent experience in pastoral counselling, especially in the United States of America, has provided a number of important insights into the way in which people can be helped. The experts in the subject seek to base their techniques on a general system of principles which are consonant with the Christian Faith, and the writers are for the most part committed Christians themselves. But they do not always avoid the trap of subjectivism: their technique sometimes appears to become more important than the external truth to which it ought to lead. The result is sometimes exaggerated statements such as— "To know oneself is to know God."[1] The truth which the writer is trying to express is valid so far as it goes, but to put it in such a bald form is to lay him open to a charge of a heretical doctrine of immanence, or even of pantheism.

It certainly can be accepted that knowledge of oneself teaches many truths about God, and that knowledge of God can be and is acquired through an understanding of his creation and especially of the human personality which he has made. But it is even more important to grasp that knowledge of oneself can only come in right perspective when it springs out of contact with and apprehension of God himself. To know God, even in the limited form available to men, is immensely more than to know oneself, and anything which tends to minimize this is dangerous from a spiritual point of view.

Moreover, to know oneself is much more than to have discovered a number of facts about oneself which had hitherto been hidden. Such facts can be revealed by such techniques as psychoanalysis. At the end of psychoanalysis a man certainly knows much more about himself than he knew before, but he may be no nearer to knowing himself in the essence of his nature and personality. This point is brought out well by Paul Tournier:

There was a time when legend, poetry and music counted for more than science in the making of a cultivated man. Doubtless it was a

[1] Carroll A. Wise, *Pastoral Counseling*, p. 162.

more humane age than ours is. Much of what we know to-day about man, not only about his body, but about the psychological and sociological laws that govern his life, was unknown. Yet it is probably true to say that man was known better then than now.[1]

This is the remark of an experienced and practising psychiatrist, and recognizes a truth of great importance for every person.

He puts it in another way when speaking of the achievements and limitations of psychoanalysis:

Psychological analysis, of course, does nothing to remove the contradictions of the human heart. Psychoanalysts would be the first to admit this. Their methods are only a way of treating inhibitions and serious psychical disturbances, a means of giving back to their patients some capacity for happiness, for normal activity and social life. But after months, and even years of analytic treatment they remain, like you and me, full of complexes, inner conflicts and ambivalent tendencies.[2]

It is commonly assumed to-day that modern writers are the first to have grappled seriously with the problems of the human personality. It is true that modern psychology has introduced new methods of examining the problems, and has thrown important new light upon them in various respects. But the problems themselves are as old as the human race, and have been the subject of much thought and experiment in earlier centuries. The teachings of the masters of the spiritual life are just as relevant now as they were when they were given, because they are the outcome of empiric examination and experiment. They are sometimes expressed in terms which are unfamiliar to our generation, but this does not affect the truths which they express. It is one of the most powerful of modern temptations to assume that everything we are discovering anew had been overlooked by our predecessors.

Modern insights have, therefore, to be related to those which have been known before and handed down to us in Christian writers of the past. It is often assumed by the moderns that anything which bears the name Christian must necessarily reflect a rigid dogmatic approach which is unsuitable for modern

[1] *The Meaning of Persons*, p. 13.   [2] Op. cit., p. 60.

methods. In pastoral counselling all the stress is often put on "staying with the patient" in the sense of avoiding any kind of judgement or the imposition of standards of a predetermined kind from without. This is an important understanding of how to deal with persons, for, as has been often noticed, an attempt to force the person concerned into a predetermined mould will at one stroke end the possibility of helping him in any way. Nevertheless a balance is required, and it must not be forgotten that the doctrines of the Christian Faith have themselves grown out of the actual experience of Christian persons: they are the formulations of what Christians have come to know in their own lives as underlying truths of God and man. The question of how individuals should be led to appropriate these truths in their own lives is one of techniques, but, so far as these experiences are true, the techniques must be related to those truths, and not be allowed to claim a spurious self-sufficiency, which may end in mere subjectivism.

Another quotation from Carroll A. Wise may make the point clearer. He is speaking about pastoral counselling of an individual:

> Further comment may be made at this point on the importance of the acceptance and clarification of the feelings which the individual verbalizes. Feelings are the core of the dynamics of the personality. Through feelings the individual expresses the conflicts which he experiences within himself and between himself and his world. Feelings and ego are closely identified. Our egos are very much involved in the way we feel: "I am as I feel." To accept a person's feelings is to accept him as he believes he is. To reject his feelings or to disapprove feelings is to reject or disapprove him as he experiences himself. This forces him to be defensive. Acceptance and clarification give a person opportunity to discover and accept himself as he is.[1]

This quotation exhibits a method of approach which is common among those dealing with these problems. What one has to notice is that, so far as the statements deal with the technique of handling the patient (or whatever he may be called: "Counselee" is too distasteful to be encouraged!), they are very sound and helpful. But when they stray into general statements of the

[1] Op. cit., p. 80.

45

nature of the person they are often unsound. It is not clear in the above extract whether the author approves of the remark "I am as I feel", but, if he does, he is far off the right track. A man may believe that he is as he feels, but one object of the Christian Faith is to assure him that such is not the case.

On the other hand it is true, as this author and others point out, that God does not deal with people as an external force, applying the stick when displeased and rewarding with candy when satisfied. He works through the laws of the personality, himself entering into the person, and gradually teaching his followers that it is in the full flowering of their personalities according to the law of their own nature, which he created, that they will find him and the fullness of life which he wants them to have. It is their emphasis on this side of the truth which makes the contributions of the newer writers on pastoral counselling of great value and importance to-day.

But the principle itself is not new. It has been taught for centuries by all the great teachers of the Faith. It is the heart of the teaching of St Thomas Aquinas about the objective and subjective ends of man, and it has been expounded in various forms by dozens of writers. The Protestant tradition, however, which combines the theory of total depravity on the one hand and an over-emphasis on the importance of the conversion experience on the other has often thrown things out of proportion.

If we frankly face the position to-day we find a state of affairs where feelings are often thought to be the most important thing, though they ought not to be in a properly balanced life. We are faced with the difficulty of putting this condition right and escaping from the tyranny of the feelings without making matters worse. In doing so we must make a clear distinction between what is in general the right way of looking at the subject, and the particular course which has to be taken when dealing with the individual person. In order to escape from the tyranny of the feelings, it is of no use merely to stress the importance of escaping. For those who suffer from this emotional tyranny, help must be given to them where they are and they must be led away from it, and gradually taught to overcome it.

But at the same time a true balance must be expounded, and an approach to the spiritual life must be taught which will help everyone to learn to lean upon God and to submit to him, and thus to get into perspective their own temporary feelings and desires. Of course feelings have a place in the full life of the human person, and if they were to be banished altogether (which incidentally is impossible) it would be an impoverishment of the personality as God has made and redeemed it. It is the dictatorship of the feelings which is disastrous, for it means the surrender of the will to the passing emotions of one's own personality, and is therefore essentially self-centred and selfish.

This point has been put admirably by Thomas Merton:

> Spiritual life is not mental life. It is not thought alone. Nor is it, of course, a life of sensation, a life of feeling—"feeling" and experiencing the things of the spirit, and the things of God.
>
> Nor does the spiritual life exclude thought and feeling. It needs both. It is not just a life concentrated at the "high point" of the soul, a life from which the mind and the imagination and the body are excluded. If it were so few people could lead it. And again, if that were the spiritual life, it would not be a life at all. If man is to live, he must be all alive, body, soul, mind, heart, spirit. Everything must be elevated and transformed by the action of God, in love and faith.[1]

We find, then, that rejection, and still more repression, of the feelings and emotions is harmful and dangerous, as modern psychologists constantly point out. Feelings have to be accepted, but this is not the same thing as saying that they have to be approved. They have to be accepted as the raw material of our personal life out of which it is God's will that something great and infinite is to be fashioned. "Acceptance" is a key concept, and one which has been recognized throughout Christian thinking and teaching for many centuries. It is based on the New Testament discovery that Christ died for us while we were yet sinners, and that God so loved the world that he gave his only-begotten Son to save it. Such words may sound like a platitude, but they contain the kernel of the matter.

[1] *Thoughts in Solitude*, p. 29.

Christianity is based on the fact of God's acceptance of us *as we are*, with all our sins and mixed-up feelings. God does not say, "When you are a good boy you may come in", but he runs to meet the sinner and puts on a feast, and the best robe and the music and dancing, although the prodigal is still in the rags of sin and has spent everything in riotous living. It is this acceptance by God, and by ourselves, which plays a key part in our spiritual life when we come to God, for we must lay ourselves open before him as we are, in all our deplorable mess, knowing that from there he will remake us into new men. And as we realize our acceptance by God, we learn through this to accept ourselves, including our feelings, and we can begin work on our lives to make them conform to what God wants them to be.

Even a slight reading of modern psychological work reveals that our feelings spring out of all kinds of places where we cannot control them, and that for the most part we are unconscious of their origin. We are not, therefore, wholly responsible for them in the first place: we are not called to account for having feelings, whether right or wrong, but merely for what we do with them when they arrive. There is unanimous testimony from the saints and the spiritual writers that feelings are no test of true prayer, either of its reality or of its success, and that they should not therefore be permitted to decide our course of action in prayer or in life. The central aspect of the personality is the will, as we have previously seen, that is, our power of choice by which we determine the course of our life and the standards and values which are to control it. Such choice is also the root of the act of love, which, when exercised, is found essentially to reside in the choice of the will.

The common view that love is not dependent on the will springs from a distorted view of the nature of love, and is fundamentally unchristian. For it makes love depend on emotional satisfaction, on what we feel we get out of it. But love is the will to give oneself to another, and even on the human scale it is far more than the satisfaction of the feelings. To separate love from the will is to make it a little thing. The teaching of Christ is plainly that love consists in the readiness for self-sacrifice for the person who is loved. We know that God loved us because he gave his Son, that this love was proved in the self-sacrifice of Jesus in life and death. Therefore, our whole effort in trying to love God may be summed up by saying that it is an attempt to unite our will to his, independently of what we may feel at any particular moment. So all the saints tell us, and so we have to learn ourselves. The history of the advance of the soul to God is the story of God teaching the person to love him independently of what he feels.

It is this conviction that causes the great writers to stress the importance of loving God in pain and suffering, so that while we thank God for what they call consolations—that is pleasant feelings—the act of love is independent of them. They all point out what is confirmed in modern psychology that feelings may have a good or a bad source, and are therefore unreliable as guides. "But all such manner of feelings may be good, wrought by a good angel, and they may be deceivable, feigned by a wicked angel, when he transfigureth him into an angel of light."[1] In the same vein Hilton says elsewhere, "thou shalt hold them [feelings of comfort] in thine own sight as they were right nought or little . . .", or, "Other imperfect souls that have such feelings outward and have not yet received the inward grace, it is not good to them for to rest in such feelings too mickle; but in as mickle as they help the soul to more stableness of thought in God, and to more love."[2]

Because they are not clear in their own minds on the subject, many Christian people enter into prayer with the wrong purpose, with the object of finding some sort of self-satisfaction through their feelings. This object may be expressed in various ways, and be called "religious experience" or something of that sort. But such a purpose inhibits the true motive of prayer which must always be the submission of the will to the will of God. Anything else introduces an "if" into the prayer, so as in effect to make the person say to God: "I will serve you, *if* you provide me with what I want in the way of religious emotions." St Bernard tells us: "Much more, the soul that loves God seeks for God, and

[1] Walter Hilton, *The Scale of Perfection*, p. 19. [2] Op. cit., p. 365.

49

wants no other prize. Where it is otherwise, you may be sure it is some other thing, not God, that really is the object of her love."[1]

In short there is only one legitimate aspiration in prayer and that is the aspiration for God himself. This must govern all else, and everything must be subordinated to it. The desire for emotional experiences is wrong because it substitutes for God the satisfactions of the human personality at a lower level than that on which God wishes us to live, and thus it prevents us from ever reaching the higher stages. The man who is content with a small achievement will never get higher, and the man who is content with his own feelings will never find God who is so far beyond any such small satisfactions.

The writers on the life of prayer through the ages are full of the same teaching about the feelings. From the early Eastern writers with their stress on passionlessness right through to the present day there is one consistent thread of teaching, that progress and growth in the life of prayer brings emancipation from the tyranny of the feelings and is identical with the submission of the whole personality to God through the will.

A common form of reliance on the feelings in ordinary life is the attitude of those who are irregular in their attendance at the public worship of the Church. They explain this by saying such things as—"I go when I feel like it", or "The service did not seem to be doing me any good, so I left off", or more positively, "I felt that I had great help from the service or the sermon on this or that occasion". There are many forms in which this outlook is expressed. It becomes illegitimate when such feelings are allowed to decide action.

It is evident that one of the objects of the worship of the Church is to provide the Christian with the grace and assistance of which he stands in need, and that if it does not do so it is failing in one of its objects, even though the failure may be the fault of the Christian concerned rather than that of the Church. But the worship of the Church is far more than this, and the partaking of the Christian in it is a solemn obligation for every man who wishes to follow the Lord and the practice of the Church which

[1] *On the Love of God*, vii.

stands under the command, "Do this in remembrance of me". Whether a person feels helped or not, an overriding obligation to take his share in the worship of the Church remains, both from the point of view of obedience to Christ and his Church, and because in this way the Body of Christ, the Church, is alone sanctified by Christ in its totality.

But even were the growth of the individual member the sole standard by which attendance at church was to be judged, it would still be a wrong inference to suppose that this growth depended on what the individual felt at the time. A man's feelings are not at his command: they are produced by all kinds of causes beyond his control. These causes may be psychological or physical, internal or external, remote or immediate. A man cannot control his feelings and turn them on or off at will. It must therefore follow that man, who wishes to direct his life in accordance with a reasonable and spiritual aim, must not allow it to be swayed hither and thither by feelings over which he himself has little control and which can be conjured into existence by uncontrolled causes.

These simple examples, applied to church-going, have a wider application in the life of prayer as a whole. The teachers of the prayer life all point out that one of the stages of the prayer life is the removal of pleasant feelings so that the love of God may be more purely an act of the will, and not be allowed to rely on adventitious aids which do not permit its strength to increase.

You must accustom yourself to privation: [Fénelon wrote in 1703] the great trouble it causes shows how much it is needed. It is only because we appropriate light, sweetness, and enjoyment, that it is so necessary that we should be stripped of all these things. So long as the soul clings to any consolation, it needs to be stripped thereof. Undoubtedly the God we feel to be beneficent and indulgent is still God, but it is God with His Gifts: God surrounded with darkness, privation, and desolation is God only. When a mother wants to attract her little one, she comes to him, her hands full of toys and sugarplums; but the father approaches his grown-up son without any presents. God goes still further; He veils His Face, He hides His Presence, and often only visits those He seeks to perfect through the utter darkness of simple faith. You are like a baby crying because you have missed your bonbons: God gives them to you now and then, and these ups and downs comfort the soul when it begins to be discouraged, while accustoming it at the same time to privation.[1]

The same principles are inculcated by other writers. St Thomas à Kempis points out that "a true lover of Christ, and a diligent follower of all virtue, does not fall back on comforts, nor seek such sensible sweetness; but rather prefers hard exercises, and to sustain severe labours for Christ".[2] St Francis de Sales makes a list of the different conditions in which the soul may find itself, and goes on to say that, whatever the condition is, it is necessary always "that our heart, our spirit and our will tend invariable and continually to the love of God its Creator, its saviour, its unique and sovereign good".[3] And he quotes St Paul: "Whether we live or die we are the Lord's. Who shall separate us from his love?"

The same teaching is to be found in St Teresa of Jesus, the great Spanish Carmelite.[4] She speaks of the spiritual sweetness which comes from prayer and compares it to earthly joys which may bring a parallel enjoyment. She goes on:

> It seems to me that the feelings which come to us from Divine things are as purely natural as these, except that their course is nobler, although these worldly joys are in no way bad. To put it briefly, worldly joys have their source in our own nature and end in God, whereas spiritual consolations have their source in God, but we experience them in a natural way and enjoy them as much as we enjoy those I have already mentioned, and indeed much more.

She goes on to distinguish between two kinds of experience and to point out that unpleasant experiences do not prevent the soul from approaching God.

It is particularly dangerous, she tells her readers, to try to gain spiritual consolations which are not being given—"For these consolations are supernatural, and, when the understanding ceases to act, the soul remains barren and suffers great aridity. And, as the foundation of the entire edifice is humility, the nearer we come to God, the greater must be the progress which we make in this virtue: otherwise, we lose everything."[5]

[1] *Spiritual Letters*, 55. [2] *The Imitation of Christ*, bk. ii, ch. 9.
[3] *Introduction to the Devout Life*, bk. iv, ch. 13.
[4] E.g., *Interior Castle*, 4th Mansions, ch. 1. [5] *Life*, ch. 12.

The above quotations from the works of great masters come from their treatment of progress in the life of prayer, but they enunciate principles which apply throughout the spiritual life. So it is that they can illuminate the first as well as the last steps on that road. But yet another warning should be heeded here. If we say, rightly, that the will and not the feelings is the determining factor in a truly Christian life, we must beware of thinking of the will in a self-centred instead of God-centred way. It is possible to think of the will as though its exercise was a matter of gritting the teeth and concentrating in a determined effort of self will. But such a concept is merely a subtle method of introducing the emotions into the will itself and thus undoing the benefit of the light which has been thrown upon it.

The choice which the will makes is all important, but its first task is submission, not inflation: the place of the human will is summed up in the Lord's Prayer—"Thy will be done". It is more a question of direction than of conscious effort. The will is rightly exercised in the choice of what is to be the dominating element in life, even if it is not often fully achieved, but a man cannot advance in the spiritual life by hauling himself up by his own boot straps by an act of will. A modern American writer, Thomas R. Kelly, puts it in this way: "Don't grit your teeth and clench your fists and say 'I will! I will!' Relax. Take hands off. Submit yourself to God. Learn to live in the passive voice—a hard saying for Americans—and let life be willed through you. For 'I will' spells not obedience."[1]

He does not of course mean to say that "I will" in response to the call of God does not spell obedience, but he condemns the utterance of the words in a spirit of self-reliance and determination which forgets that the first step of obedience is submission to the will of God and the reception of his grace and help in the measure which he is pleased to give. Perhaps Jeremy Taylor may be allowed to sum it up: "Let zeal be seated in the will and choice, and regulated with prudence and a sober understanding, not in the fancies and affections; for these will make it full of noise and empty of profit, but that will make it deep and smooth, material and devout."[2]

[1] A Testament of Devotion, p. 56.   [2] Holy Living, ch. 4, sec. 3.

A modern book by two Roman Catholics has put succinctly the main point about the attitude of a Christian towards his feelings. The writers deal mainly with the issue of moral responsibility in the light of compulsive and other strong feelings which arise from the unconscious.

> Moral responsibility lies chiefly in the way we manage our feelings, and the way they affect others around us—*not* in the "goodness" or "badness" of the feelings themselves. So many Catholics are overwhelmed with guilt because they feel angry or resentful. To attempt to deny such feeling is to deny a part of human nature itself. It should be a chief concern of the confessor to help the individual see himself and his emotions as they are; with patient self-acceptance comes the desire and the ability to channel the more unruly feelings into healthy safety valves so as not to hurt the sensibility of others, or interfere unjustly with their lives.
>
> A mother can be helped to accept the negative feelings which every parent sometimes has towards her children. Children can be shown that it is natural to "hate" their mother or father on occasion. Adults, in their relationships with each other, must learn to resign themselves to inevitable clashes of temperaments, opinions and preferences. A mutual and genuine respect for individual human differences is the key to the resolution of routine personality clashes. So often a person becomes angry at himself for being angry at others. This is a double dose of anger, which makes the problem twice as difficult to manage. (This may explain why a man with a bad temper can almost never laugh at himself.) If an individual is able to accept, and occasionally even smile at, his own negative and hostile feelings, he will be far better able to make allowances for the similar feelings of others towards himself.[1]

This quotation was written with the particular duties in mind of those hearing Confessions, but it has far wider application. It deals with anger and resentment between human personalities, yet the principles apply to other aspects of the Christian life, not only in the matter of moral responsibility but in that of growth and understanding in the spiritual life. The attitude depicted by the writers as desirable in dealing with the emotions or feelings is basic to a healthy spiritual life and a proper understanding of its nature.

[1] G. Hagmaier and R. W. Gleason, *Moral Problems Now*, p. 61.

6

Self-discipline

That there is need for some kind of training in the spiritual life ought to be clear both from the New Testament and from the great Christian teachers throughout the centuries. Yet many Christians give almost no thought to the matter, or allow it to depend on the bits and pieces which they absorb from sermons. The sermons should, of course, be received attentively, but they do not normally provide opportunities great enough to do more than indicate some general principles. Every Christian ought to be giving the question of spiritual training careful and sustained thought.

Jesus himself sets a plain example to his followers. Not only did he spend many years in preparation before he began his own ministry of teaching, preaching, and healing, but during it he often put aside times for solitude and prayer. His ministry began with fasting and prayer in the wilderness; he often withdrew into a place apart for meditation and prayer; he willingly and deliberately accepted hardship and mortification as part of his work. He constantly emphasized the importance of these elements in the lives of his followers, speaking of the need to take up the cross, to engage in prayer, to follow him. There can be no dispute that these elements form an important part of the attitude of Jesus as we find it in the Gospels.

St Paul teaches the same principles. He speaks of the Christian life as being like a race, for which Christians must go into serious training like those who compete in the Olympic Games. He tells his readers that he bruises his body and keeps it in subjection, lest after he has preached to others, he himself should be a castaway (1 Cor. 9.27). He gives a vast list of the sufferings which he has undergone, and is still prepared to undergo, as part of his duty in preaching the Gospel. The readiness to suffer for their Lord is a common feature of all the New Testament writers, and it is seen as part of the preparation for their future glory.

All this is commonplace and could be easily established with many quotations: there is nothing new in referring to it. In the light of the evidence it is only remarkable that so few Christians take what they read seriously and try to apply it to their own lives. For many Christians, not merely of the nominal type, religion is too often regarded as a useful aid to living, something to which they can turn for comfort and strength when the ordinary conditions of everyday life become difficult. They regard it frequently not as a preparation, a stern training for the future, but as something essentially connected with this life, the success of which is to be judged by its efficiency in getting them over the hurdles of their worldly living. One can only say that this attitude of mind is completely at variance with that of the New Testament and early Church.

Training in the spiritual life is seen in the New Testament to consist of two different elements. First, there are the steps which a Christian takes to order his own life so as to bring it into accord with the call of Christ. This is shown in St Paul's words about beating under his body and bringing it into subjection. Fasting, self-discipline, and rule are the means by which this is done, and they must be found in some measure in the life of every person who is serious about his Christian profession.

Secondly, there are the mortifications and sufferings which come upon a person from without. St Paul in his second letter to the Corinthians (11.23 and following) specifies some of the hardships which he has undergone for his Lord and his Faith—beatings, shipwreck, dangerous journeys, hunger and thirst, cold, and exposure. And after detailing these sufferings he goes on to speak of "a thorn given me in the flesh . . . to harass me, to keep me from being too elated" (2 Cor. 12.7). All these he sees as part of the mortification which he has to undergo in the process of spreading the Gospel. And we must remember that spreading the Gospel was and is the main aim of every true Christian. We cannot be interested in a kind of soul culture for its own sake, though some writing on the spiritual life has given this impression. A Christian knows that his own life has meaning only in so far as he participates in the work of redemption, begun by Jesus Christ. It is this work of redemption into which a Christian has been incorporated by baptism—that is the whole meaning of the sacrament. That is why evangelism is not an optional extra for a Christian, it is part of his being, which has been redeemed by Christ and incorporated into his Church.

Perhaps we may dwell on this point a little longer, because it brings out the truth which prevents the one-sided and self-centred from taking command of the spiritual life. When considering growth in prayer it is necessary to abstract one part of the spiritual life from the rest and to speak of it as though it was all that mattered. And in one way it *is* all that matters, but it does not stand alone, and this fact must be continually brought to mind to avoid a lack of balance and truth. We do not suppose that it is possible for a Christian to live his life without any desire to enjoy the blessings which God has promised to those that love him. On the contrary a wish to partake in such joys is a natural and proper part of the Christian outlook. Jesus himself makes this clear in his own teachings, where the subject of future rewards and punishments not infrequently occurs.

In our consideration of the spiritual life we are frankly considering what is best for us, how we should do the best with our lives, and grow in that way which God has provided for us. But at the same time we must be perfectly clear that this is not the main object of our life—merely to enjoy the blessings which God gives to his children. These blessings are, so to speak, the offshoot of something else, namely the doing of the will of God. This is the paradox of the Christian life, and indeed of the life of love even in less exalted conditions, that he who seeks his own satisfaction first, does not find it. He only finds fullness of life who seeks the will of God. "Seek ye first the kingdom of God and all these things shall be added unto you." (Matt. 6.33.) Jesus makes it clear that this insight is basic to the Christian life. "He that findeth his life shall lose it, and he that loseth his life for my sake shall find it." (Matt. 10.39.) In such sayings as this, but above all in the whole pattern of his life, sufferings, and death, Jesus reveals the fundamental principles of the spiritual life.

We find our fulfilment, then, by giving ourselves away in love to God. Perhaps "fulfilment" is a better word in this connection than "happiness" because it has less of a feeling of self-enjoyment, though it is clear that only in fulfilment can true happiness be found. In committing ourselves wholly to God and preparing ourselves as well as we can to be capable of fulfilling our tasks and opportunities, we at the same time commit ourselves to the whole operation of God, which Jesus came to inaugurate afresh with his life and death. This operation is the work of redeeming mankind, of bringing it back to God through the revelation of love which Jesus has given and through the power which he has revealed. That means that there can be no such commitment, no incorporation of the Christian into Christ and the Church, except in so far as he is also incorporated into the work of redeeming mankind which is the sole object of the exercise.

The question, therefore, before the Christian layman is not whether or not he has any responsibility for evangelism, but whether or not he is in fact a Christian. For it is impossible to claim the name "Christian", still less really to be one, without being wholly committed to do the work of him who sent Jesus and now calls us to the same work. To think that a man can be a Christian without being fully involved in the work of redeeming mankind, is like thinking that one can hold a commission in the Army without being involved in defending one's country—the two things are conterminous.

This has repercussions on training in the spiritual life. For, while such training has the purpose of making one spiritually fit, it is only done so that we may be fit for something, able to do something, namely to exercise our powers in the service of God and in doing his will. We are not like men who every day keep themselves fit in their gymnasium so that they may eat more comfortably, sleep more soundly, and enjoy swimming in their private bathing pool. We are like men who have undertaken a strenuous course of training so that they may be efficient soldiers, or spiritual Commandos, and be ready to do what is required when the need comes. As a side result these men find themselves thoroughly fit and experience a new enjoyment in being in this condition.

This perspective is important for spiritual health, since one of the things which most easily ruins the life of the spirit is the self-centredness or self-satisfaction which can so easily creep in unawares. When this happens it rots the spiritual life at the roots and induces a form of spiritual self-centredness which is thoroughly unpleasant. *Corruptio optimi pessima*, the corruption of the best thing is the worst, is a truth which is clearly seen in such situations.

There have been periods in Christian history when the teaching about mortification or self-denial has been very severe, and, one must judge, somewhat exaggerated. It is not surprising that during the course of Christian history all kinds of emphases have been found: at one end has been the wearing of hair shirts, and incredible hardships in the desert, such as those practised by St Simeon Stylites, who lived on the top of a pillar without ever coming down for a period of more than forty years, engaged in adoration and intercession; at the other extreme we meet Christians who reject the whole idea of mortification as an unwarranted invention of monks and such like people. The true attitude lies between the extremes, as is so often the case. Certainly the "novel austerity" as the *Dictionary of the Christian Church* describes the actions of St Simeon Stylites is not likely to attract Christians to-day, when someone only sits on top of a pillar in order to break a record, though none has yet come within striking distance of St Simeon. But conditions in his day were very different from ours now, and it is worth remembering that the influence of the saint on the pillar was very considerable in promoting the cause of Christianity in various ways. And if we in our day consider his particular form of austerity somewhat odd, it is worth noting that God saw fit to make use of it.

In the twentieth century the danger is not of too much, but of too little, austerity. In large areas of Christendom even those days of fasting and abstinence which the Church lays down are imperfectly observed or overlooked altogether. In seeking the true Christian attitude to self-discipline we shall look for guidance from the masters of the spiritual life, whose experience and influence have been most widely recognized by those who know them.

Let us consider first the question of voluntary self-discipline, imposed without necessity. It is certain that all Christians need some discipline of this sort, and that it ought to be expressed in the form of a rule. The proper organization of the life of a Christian requires that it be ordered by a deliberate act of choice, and not left to the whims of hour to hour. For example, no Christian ought to be without some rule of prayer. It is not necessary that a rule be very strenuous—indeed it is often better that it should not be so. But some rule is indispensable, if prayer is to take its proper part in everyday life. There must be some rule about receiving the sacraments, about reading the Bible, about the observance of days of fasting, about almsgiving, and other things. It is not our purpose here to try to provide a rule for everyone, for that would be bound to fail since circumstances differ so much in people's lives. But we ought to give some thought to the principles which should underlie such rule.

The most important is perhaps that a rule should be a minimum and not a maximum. This is another way of saying that a rule should be kept if it is made, and it should not, therefore, be too hard, otherwise once it is broken there will be a strong temptation to throw over the whole thing. It can be increased as progress is made, but it should err on the side of laxity rather than strictness. But the rule should be there, for it is to form the basis on which the spiritual life will rest, and give a sort of framework to the rest of one's activities. It should take into account the subjects just mentioned, and others where there is need to make some special effort of control.

It is desirable that any rule should be discussed with someone else, preferably a spiritual counsellor, or consultant, or director, who can give an outside opinion as to the wisdom of the rule and as to its completeness. It is difficult to prescribe spiritual remedies for oneself, just as it is difficult to treat oneself physically without occasional recourse to the physician. It is well to consult those who have some experience of spiritual health.

Christians vary a good deal in their readiness to go to their ministers to discuss such matters. In the Roman and Orthodox Churches where the practice of confession is common, an opportunity is thus provided for advice. In Anglican circles there has been an increase of this practice and also in some Protestant Churches, where the habit of pastoral counselling has been increasing and has proved to be of very great help in emotional and spiritual problems. The need for a spiritual adviser is stressed by most of the writers on the spiritual life, who deal with the matter explicitly, and it has to be remembered that most of them took the existence of the director for granted in the life of anyone who was seriously trying to develop his spiritual life.

K. E. Kirk provides one of the reasons for spiritual consultation in writing—

> Cassian (Collat. ii. 14, 15) makes the interesting observation that the Holy Spirit is not wont to reveal directly to men anything that may be learnt through human teachers. Thus Samuel, though directly called by the Holy Spirit, must go to Eli for an interpretation of the voice. Saul, on the Damascus Road, is converted by the vision of our Lord "yet Almighty God, notwithstanding that He sees him so well disposed, does not disclose His designs." And why? Because there is in Damascus a priest, Ananias by name, to whom he can make application. "Go to him", says our Lord, "and learn from him what I will have you to do."[1]

Not only does the Church provide everyday opportunities for guidance through its clergy and others, but its own history is rich in literature which can prove of great assistance to those who want direction and illumination. But in finding what is most suitable for any particular person the guidance of someone who knows both the literature and the person concerned is desirable. St Francis de Sales in describing a "short method to know God's will"[2] points out that it is necessary to show great humility and not to think that an answer to the question we are asking can be

---

[1] *Some Principles of Moral Theology*, p. 134 n.
[2] *Treatise on the Love of God*, bk. viii, ch. 14.

forced out of God. He tells his readers that besides thought and prayer "the counsel of our director, and perhaps, of two or three other spiritual persons" should be sought, and it is on the basis of such consultation that the decision must be made.

The dangers of remaining solitary are pointed out by St Teresa:

> We err in thinking that we need only know that we must keep our thoughts fixed on Thee. We do not understand that we should consult those better instructed than ourselves, nor are we aware that there is anything for us to learn. We pass through terrible trials on account of not understanding our own nature and take what is not merely harmless, but good, for a grave fault.[1]

She goes on to point out that we cannot stop the working of the natural order, "neither can we control our imagination". If we do not understand what is the real importance of our existence we may think ourselves to be completely divorced from God when in fact we are close to him. For such conditions the help of an experienced director is essential.

"Do you wish in good earnest to set out on the way of devotion?" asks St Francis de Sales in another place, "Seek out some good man who will guide and direct you. This is the counsel of counsels."[2] It would be an exaggeration to say that no one can progress in the spiritual life without consulting others. God can provide for any person in what way he wills, but it is clear that his normal method is through those who have become qualified by study and experience to give advice. It is not for us to expect God to vary his methods for our convenience when normal channels of help are open to us.

A good director or adviser will be particularly useful in any doubts about the measure of self-discipline which we ought to adopt in a particular case. The enthusiasms of certain ages and conditions lead some to want to throw themselves into mortification in far too strict a way, whereas others through repressed emotions and influences from their past life seek in exaggerated discipline to find satisfaction for their emotions, which they do not recognize when making their resolutions.

[1] *Interior Castle*, 4th Mansions, ch. 1, para. 9.
[2] *Introduction to the Devout Life*, pt. 1, ch. 4.

Before going further into this point we must note that there are wide differences between saints about what is desirable and necessary in the way of mortification. We have already had occasion to refer to the unusual austerities of St Simeon Stylites, and there would be general agreement that his particular methods would not be suitable for the twentieth century. We find also in some saints, such as the Blessed Henry Suso, fearful self castigation which could not possibly be recommended, and some of the desert fathers exhibit similar tendencies. But though we find these attitudes on one wing, we find a different outlook among the greatest teachers of the spiritual life. Spiritual men and holy women were not all free from emotional disturbances and in some cases almost pathological conditions, and we are not called to take such persons as our own models. What made such people saints and leaders was not the austerities which they undertook, sometimes undesirably, but the fact that they were able to use the raw material of their own personalities in the service of God. As often happens, many of those who saw them confused their devotion to God with the outward austerities which they were known to have adopted.

In approaching these questions it is sensible to apply to them knowledge which has come to us through recent study of psychology, itself a gift from God to help our development and growth. It is also important that we should apply to any particular course of action the test of whether it has earned the general approval of the Church. This is not to be found in pronouncements by some ecclesiastical authority, but in discovering what has commended itself to the best exponents of the spiritual life over the centuries. And when these two tests are made it is found that exaggerated forms of self-discipline and very severe mortification are not generally approved by the spiritual masters.

At this point it is important to see the relation between self-discipline and the way in which the normal trials of everyday life are met. It is quite impossible for anyone to live a normal life in the world without constantly meeting difficulties, problems of personal relationships, trials of all kinds, which must be faced each day. This is the ordinary material which is given to each one of us for the formation of the Christian life. Out of it we have to find the will of God in every aspect of our life. A distinguished non-juror, Robert Nelson, made this point: "Conform your self to the will of God in those afflictions which he sends you."[1] He goes on to point out that there are some who are quite ready— or think themselves to be—to face suffering which they choose themselves, but who show themselves unwilling to take what comes to them in the normal course of events. "Ought you to prescribe to Him the particular cross he should lay upon you? Banish all such thoughts from your mind, and let the cross which He sends you, be received with resignation and satisfaction, though it may be it is not what you would have chosen for your self."

More modern writers say the same thing. Evelyn Underhill puts it forcefully: "In general, the mortifications sent by God and the ordinary friction of existence are enough to discipline our souls. Voluntary mortifications are *never* to be assumed till the necessary difficulties and contradictions of life are cheerfully and fully accepted."[2] In a later letter she drives home the same lesson: "As to self-abnegation: be ready to accept every mortification and sacrifice God asks of you in unruffled peace—but No Cross-Hunting!"[3]

This note is found in the writers of many centuries. Mother Harriet Monsell, a nineteenth-century Anglican Mother Superior, speaks the same language as the saints. "As regards fasting", she wrote in a letter, "do what you can in simple ways. Fix on three definite acts of self-denial, one as regards food, one as regards words, one as regards habits of self-indulgence, and watch carefully about these points, being very faithful to your resolve. Try little things, not great things. Little things very faithfully done, will advance you on your way more than great efforts in which you would break down."[4]

In emphasizing the danger of extremism in devotion Lorenzo Scupoli writes that there are many who by indulging in it have ended far worse than they began, like the man in the parable into

[1] *The Practice of True Devotion*, ch. 7, sec. 8.   [2] *Letters*, p. 193.
[3] Op. cit., p. 326.   [4] T. T. Carter, *Harriet Monsell*, p. 157.

whom seven devils entered. "This has been the end of many, who, following presumptuously the impulse of an indiscreet zeal, have, in their excessive outward austerities, gone beyond the measure of their own virtue, and so have perished in their own inventions, and become the sport of malicious fiends."[1] And he ends the chapter with these words : "I would say further, that in the pursuit of inward holiness, as well as of outward devotion, we should proceed with some moderation, as has been shown above on the subject of the gradual acquisition of virtues."

/ The conclusion is clear, namely that, if special mortifications and austerities are to be used, it must be only after advice from a qualified person and must never precede or replace the right dealing with the obstacles and difficulties of everyday life. Sometimes the adoption of austerities can even be a means of trying to escape from the very conditions in which we have been placed, all of which must be regarded as opportunities which have been provided for our own progress in spiritual growth with the help of God.

But this does not mean that there is to be no rule of life. On the contrary the acceptance of a rule of life, preferably in consultation with a good adviser, is an indispensable element in the control and offering to God of everyday living, and together with the trials already referred to, is to form the basic ground on which our life in Christ is to be built.

[1] *The Spiritual Combat*, ch. 42.

7

Two Aspects of Love
[*Agape* and *Eros*]

In recent years there has been much discussion of two aspects of love, represented by the two Greek words *agape* (ἀγάπη) and *eros* (ἔρως). The classic examination of this theme was made by Dr Anders Nygren, then Professor at Lund University and afterwards Bishop of Lund, in his book published in Swedish under the title, *The Christian thought of love* (*Den kristna kärlekstanken*). This work, translated into English with the title, *Agape and Eros*, contains a detailed analysis of the meaning of these two Greek words, which are both translated "love" in English.

More recently C. S. Lewis in a little book entitled *The Four Loves* identifies *eros* with love between the sexes, a much narrower interpretation than Nygren gives to the word. The wider meaning must be preferred and will be followed in this short discussion. It is of course impossible adequately to summarize the arguments and learning of Dr Nygren's work in a few words, but, as his conclusions are of importance to any treatment of Christian prayer, some attempt must be made to consider his conclusions.

His general thesis is that *eros* is love or desire from a human standpoint and is Greek and pre-Christian in origin. There is, therefore, nothing specifically Christian about it. With the New Testament, however, an altogether new idea of love is found which is expressed by the word *agape*. He points out that *agape* is spontaneous and uncaused, that it is indifferent to human merit, that it is creative, and that it opens the way to fellowship with God. He goes on to stress that in his view the two conceptions of love reveal "a fundamental, all-embracing opposition" and that they are "the symbols of two completely opposite

66

attitudes to life, two utterly different religious and ethical types. They represent two streams which run through the whole history of religion, the egocentric and the theocentric outlook".

Perhaps the point can best be made by quoting the scheme which the author himself provides to set out the essential opposition in summary form (Vol. I, p. 165):

1. *Eros* is a desire of good for the self
   Agape is a self-giving

2. *Eros* is man's effort to ascend
   Agape comes down from above

3. *Eros* is man's way to God
   Agape is God's way to man

4. *Eros* is man's achievement, the endeavour of man to achieve salvation
   Agape is a free gift, a salvation which is the work of Divine love

5. *Eros* is egocentric love, a form of self-assertion of the highest, sublimest kind
   Agape is unselfish love, which "seeketh not its own" and freely spends itself

6. *Eros* seeks to gain its life, a life Divine, immortal
   Agape lives by God's life, and therefore dares to "lose it"

7. *Eros* is a will to have and to possess, resting on a sense of need
   Agape freely gives and spends, for it rests on God's own richness and fulness

8. *Eros* is primarily human love, and God is the object of Eros
   Agape is primarily God's own love, for God is *Agape*

9. *Eros*, when it is applied to God, is a love fashioned after the pattern of human love
   Agape, when it appears in man, is a love that takes its form from God's own love

10. *Eros* is determined by and dependent on the quality of its object, its beauty and value; hence it is not spontaneous but "caused", called forth by the value of its object
    Agape is sovereign and independent with regard to its object, and is poured out on "the evil and the good"; hence it is spontaneous, "uncaused", and bestows itself on those who are not worthy of it

11. *Eros* recognizes value in its object, and therefore loves it
    Agape loves, and creates value in its object.

Dr Nygren sums up: "No real synthesis was possible between two ideas so completely opposite: *Eros*, which starts from the sense of human need, and seeks God in order to satisfy man's spiritual yearnings, and *Agape*, which freely pours itself out in the richness of Divine Grace. If a reconciliation between these two is apparently reached, it is certain that *Agape* has been betrayed."

This is strong language, and we may readily and thankfully admit that Dr Nygren's work provides an emphasis of real value for Christians, when he is discussing and explaining the nature of *Agape*. But where his conclusions are negative he is on much less firm ground. The general impression left by his book is that all efforts to order prayer or advance in prayer savour of *eros*, and must, therefore, be condemned as sub-Christian. In his first preface to the translation of Volume I, Fr A. G. Hebert, s.s.m., seemed partly to endorse this view: "Hence arises the conception of the Catholic system as a way of works and a pursuit of perfection, by which the individual attains to holiness and ascends to God; connected with this is the following of the way of mysticism, concerning which Dr Nygren's pertinent remarks provide much food for thought."

These problems are fundamental and must be dealt with if a firm foundation is to be found on which to proceed. What Dr Nygren does not seem to do is to relate to his theology of *agape* in redemption a natural theology or theology of creation. Fr Hebert sees this and notes it in his preface. If we accept that the contrast exists between *agape* and *eros* we are no further in condemning one or praising the other. Nor by proving *agape* to be New Testament and *eros* to be pre-Christian is it possible to decide anything about *eros* at all as far as its place in human life or its relation to God is concerned. Professor Nygren's conclusions as to the nature of *agape* may readily be granted, and they should be kept continually in mind.

But what of *eros*? It must not be thought that the human soul can return to God or ever come near to God by its own efforts. But God made man in creation, and the creation is the act of God's love, that *agape* of which Dr Nygren so eloquently speaks. Man was made to love and serve God and to live in union with him. God's love is eternal and cannot be confined to the act of redemption in Christ Jesus. It is in Christ certainly that his love is completely expressed and fully active, but it was the same God who created the world by an act of the same love (*agape*) by which we are saved. "*Agape* is creative", writes Professor Nygren, "that which in itself is without value acquires value by the fact that it is the object of God's love." That is true, and it means that every human soul has infinite value because each is created by God's love. Therefore to say "that the idea of the infinite value of the human soul is not a basic Christian idea at all" seems somewhat off the mark. In human history the idea of the immortality of the soul appears before Christ, but that does not affect its Christian character in the fuller light that we receive from the Incarnation.

This raises another point. To say that an idea or a practice is Greek in origin, or from any other pre-Christian source, does not mean that it is necessarily non-Christian or sub-Christian. "This is the true light which lighteth every man that cometh into the world." (John 1.9.) There is a natural revelation which is no less from God because it is before Christ, although every supposed truth must be rigorously tested in the light of Christ's revelation. The Christian Gospel enables us to see these other discoveries in their true perspective. God was in the world before Christ, as St Paul implied when he wrote, "when the time had fully come God sent forth his Son" (Gal. 4.4). Christians should be ready to appreciate those contributions from outside their own borders which enrich their understanding of God's ways which are "past finding out".

In the teaching of the Christian writers on prayer there are two sides to every question. One side—the most important by far—is God's way to man, his grace, and his love. The other side is man's soul, his spiritual activities and progress, which is equally indispensable in any thought on the subject at all. It is irrational to suppose that man is not to learn from his experience of God in prayer and in daily life, just as it is irrational to profess total agnosticism. Such an attitude ignores much of the work commonly attributed to the Holy Spirit, and denies God's power to enlighten man. When writers on the spiritual life speak of man's side of the question their language is bound to be reminiscent of the heresy which Lutherans abhor more than any other—Pelagianism. But this language is balanced by their teaching on grace, and must not be taken as if it stood alone. It is impossible to speak of man's activity without seeming to give ground for an accusation that an activity apart from God is meant. This is the last thing the great writers intend, as can be seen by what they say elsewhere.

In Christian teaching there are bound to be occasions where the human mind is incapable of seeing the synthesis which exists in the purpose of God. No two opinions may be held which are mutually contradictory, but there are always tensions which must be held together in order to maintain the fullness of Christian belief and the inner meaning of the Gospel. Such are the doctrines of the impassibility of God and the suffering always necessary to true love; the love and wrath of God; grace and free will; faith and works. It is not suggested that no synthesis is possible in every one of these cases, but there always remains something beyond it which is inexplicable by us now, and this is what we mean by the word "tension". This tension is found in the relations between *agape* and *eros*. But it is a one-sided and misleading theory which would have it that there is no human activity involved in love; it is just as misleading as the idea that love and prayer is nothing but human activity.

The doctrine which finds no place in the writers on prayer is that of *tota depravatio* or total depravity. There is no reason for surprise at this, for Christian teaching has never included the theory that man by the fall is completely sinful, in the sense that there is no trace left of the good desires implanted in him by God in creation. As for Anglican teaching the Article (IX) which states that "man is very far gone from original righteousness" specifically does not state that he is entirely wicked. We are indeed to hold firmly that he cannot "turn and prepare himself by his own natural strength and good works, to faith and calling upon God" (Article X). No service is done to Christianity by over-emphasizing either side of the matter.

There are many resemblances between Christian and non-Christian mysticism (the word being used to refer to efforts to reach the higher states of union with God in prayer). But this fact does not *ipso facto* condemn the Christian mystics. It is possible to take the best in the non-Christian world and turn it to the service of Christ. Thus our Lord used the Old Testament; thus St Paul says at Athens (Acts 17.23), "whom therefore ye ignorantly worship, him declare I unto you". They worship; and the object of their worship, however ignorant it may be, is God.

There is a fundamental difference between the mysticism of

Christians and of others. This difference lies in the doctrine of grace based on the Incarnation which is the very heart and root of Christian mysticism. Indeed it would be difficult to introduce a doctrine of grace into a non-Christian system without radically changing its nature and the basic ideas on which it rests. There is no need, however, to justify Christian writers in such a round-about way. No one who reads their works as a whole can doubt that the whole system stands on the basis of the grace of God, nor can he fail to see how constantly the writings of the later authors are submitted to the judgement of the Church.

Dr Nygren divides the religious types into two, the egocentric and the theocentric—a misleading categorization which encourages the reader to envisage Christianity as a religion where thought for self does not enter at all. Whence can such an idea have its origin? Certainly not in the New Testament where our Lord's teaching is quite full of rewards and punishments, which one must suppose were intended to be taken seriously and to be used by men for the purpose of directing their lives aright. There has been in this century a strong reaction against the tendency of earlier times to use fear of hell as the main motive for leading a life in accordance with Christian moral standards. No doubt such a presentation was seriously at fault, but it is wrong to say that thoughts of heaven and hell, of punishment and reward, play no part in the Christian Faith. Our Lord's teaching is the touchstone, and it is clear.

The chief motive of a Christian must be *agape*, given by God and flowing out of his life towards God and his fellow men. The more this element predominates, the more Christ-like will be a man's life, but it would be a bold man who would say that he was completely indifferent to heaven or hell. St Paul says, "For I could wish that myself were accursed from Christ for my brethren, my kinsmen according to the flesh" (Rom. 9.3), but he also says, "I am in a strait betwixt two having a desire to depart and to be with Christ; which is far better" (Phil. 1.23). Here St Paul shows both sides, the pure motive of love for others, and the equally necessary desire for himself. He could hardly have used a more "natural" word for desire than *epithumeo* (ἐπιθυμέω).

The desires of the natural man for reward are given by God in creation in order that man may seek the true reward, and *with the grace of God* attain it.

Man's desires, given to him in creation, have been misdirected through sin and cannot find their satisfaction except as a result of grace and revelation. There is no quarrel to be found with the doctrine that grace precedes good desires, though that grace may be unrecognized. But it cannot be too strenuously asserted that there is a place for desire in the Christian life, that is for a yearning for the fulfilment of the true self and for an effort to attain. This is the counterpart of God's grace and revelation.

What then is God's attitude (if we may so speak) to these desires and efforts? In answer to this question any idea of merit must be rigidly excluded. The Lutherans have properly rebelled against the conception that man can ever be anything over against God. Man cannot claim reward from God. God grants his gifts freely out of his own nature, which is *agape*. But it is of the nature of true love that it never forces itself on any person. What is freely given must be equally freely received. The gift is offered by God, but it must be taken or received by man. Something is required in man's will before he can accept the gift, just as penitence must be present if forgiveness is to be effective. That is the key word—"effective". God's gifts take effect in the life of man where, and only where, man's attitude is commensurate to the gift. Our Lord says, "Ask and it shall be given you; seek and ye shall find; knock and it shall be opened unto you" (Luke 11.9). All is given, but before it is received there must be the asking, the seeking, and the knocking.

Jesus is teaching no doctrine of merit, but merely the meaning of the Christian doctrine of free will. The will of man is the centre of his person and until his will is given to Christ he cannot receive Christ's gifts. This point is of great importance for the will is expressed not in words, nor in feelings, but in actions. "Ye shall know them by their fruits." (Luke 7.16.) If a man's will is devoted to God the fact will inevitably appear in his life. The works of a man have no merit in themselves, they have no value before God. Their importance lies in the fact that by them the attitude of the will is proved, and on the attitude of the will depends a man's capability of receiving the gifts freely offered and given by God. This attitude may be called faith, or penitence, or devotion: it matters not, so long as the essence of the position is discerned.

The application of this to prayer is plain. God offers to all men the graces of prayer, but men do not receive such graces when they do not ask or desire them. Absolution can only be given to the penitent and the graces of prayer can only be given to the prayerful. The will to receive these graces of God is shown only in actions, that is in those actions directed towards the attainment of the end of prayer, union with God. These actions are suggested by Christian experience in the descriptions and instructions given to the Church by those who have evidently been given such graces. W. R. Inge wrote:

> On all questions *about* religion there is the most distressing divergency. But the saints do not contradict each other. They all tell the same story. They claim to have had glimpses of the land that is very far off, and they prove that they have been there by bringing back perfectly consistent and harmonious reports of it. There never was a greater mistake than to suppose that there is no authentic information, but only subjective fancies and hallucinations about the spiritual world. Subjective fancies betray their subjectivity by reflecting the idiosyncrasies of their creators, but in the higher religious experiences there is singularly little subjective distortion.[1]

It is from such saints that Christians to-day may learn what is the spirit of prayer that, with God's grace, will be completed by the gift of prayer.

Finally we should observe that in our experience the universe is *ordered* according to certain principles of cause and effect established by God in creation. This is evident in the physical and mental spheres. Is it not reasonable to suppose that there is a similar order in the realm of the spirit? The saints say that this spiritual order is a fact. Both the will of man and the gifts of God are related to the divine order through which the spiritual life is exercised and extended.

[1] *Speculum Animae*, p. 5.

8

The Biblical Background

It is not uncommon to find writing on prayer which hardly refers to the teaching of the New Testament. The reason may be that the teaching of the New Testament on the subject is not carefully indexed and arranged, but it is embedded in the material of the Gospels and Epistles and in the background against which the life of Jesus himself was lived. It would need a biblical scholar to set out in its fullness the various elements which affect Christian teaching on the life of prayer, and no such attempt will be made here; nevertheless it is important that our own study should be related to the New Testament so far as possible.

We shall, therefore, try to answer this question: What do we find of underlying principles about prayer in the New Testament and especially in the teaching of Jesus himself? There are some who would maintain that the tradition of Christian prayer as we know it in the great mystics is a betrayal of the true principles of the Gospel, and, if that were the case, it would be of the utmost importance to try to discern where and in what details the betrayal has taken place. In this matter it is important to distinguish between the life of prayer itself, and the theories about its nature which have been propounded. The latter have in some cases been difficult to reconcile with New Testament teaching and the conception of God which we meet there. Nevertheless there is no reason on that account to hold that the experiences and life of prayer themselves have been false or in any way unfaithful. Moreover in the great teachers there is no clash between their doctrines and those of the writers of the New Testament.

The main influences in the circles in which Jesus was brought up seem to have been those of the apocalyptic teachers, who emphasized the inner character of religion and its final consummation at the end of time by an act of God. This eschatological element had a number of important effects, among them a renewed stress on the importance of inner obedience to God. Jewish practices in any case encouraged the pious Jew to relate all the little events of everyday life to God, making formal acts of dedication, so as to bring the whole life into relation with God and his law. In this way a framework was provided for the practice of individual private prayer.

Moreover, the psalms provided for the Jews, as they have since provided for generations of Christians, an ideal means of expressing the longing of the individual soul for God. "Like as the hart desireth the waterbrooks, so longeth my soul after thee O God." (42.1.) How deeply moving are such expressions as these, and the psalms abound in them. They formed the stuff of the prayers of pious Jews, and gave inspiring expression to their spiritual aspirations.

In the New Testament itself we find that private prayer is taken for granted, and no question arises as to its desirability. We read that John the Baptist taught his disciples to pray. Indeed it was a reference to the prayer of the Baptist's followers that called forth the Lord's Prayer itself.

"Once, in a certain place, Jesus was at prayer. When he ceased, one of his disciples said, 'Lord, teach us to pray, as John taught his disciples.' He answered, 'When you pray, say, ...'" (Luke 11.1.) This short extract from St Luke's Gospel informs us at one time of the fact that John the Baptist taught his disciples and also that Jesus was in the habit of praying himself, and that he evidently wished his disciples to do the same. There is, however, no record of the kind of prayer which the disciples of John the Baptist used and speculation on the subject is hardly worth while.

It has been pointed out that the words of the prayer which Jesus taught his followers were all taken from Jewish sources: "The early Christian liturgy is entirely modelled on the Jewish. This is seen not only in the Lord's Prayer, which is entirely composed of parts of Jewish prayer, but also. . . ."[1] This shows

[1] *Encyclopaedia of Religion and Ethics*, vol. x, p. 193.

that the teaching of Jesus was in accordance with the general tradition of Jewish devotion, but it is in his selection and combination of Jewish elements that the genius of spiritual insight is to be found. This is certainly the case with the Lord's Prayer, to which more attention will be given a little later.

Throughout the Gospels there are constant references to the practice of Jesus withdrawing from other people and going apart to pray. Very near the beginning of St Mark's account (1.35) we read: "Very early next morning he got up and went out. He went away to a lonely spot and remained there in prayer." The same thing is recorded in Mark 4.46 just before he appeared to his disciples walking upon the lake, and later St Mark, like the other evangelists, records the prayer of Jesus in the Garden of Gethsemane as he went to his passion and death. St Luke writes (5.16): "And from time to time he would withdraw to lonely places for prayer." There are a number of other references both in St Luke and in St Matthew to the same thing, and we can be left in no doubt that it was part of the regular practice of Jesus to withdraw from the company of others in order to enter into prayer with the Father.

The example of Jesus then is clear, and not only did our Lord set this example himself, but at various times in his ministry he gave teaching which either dealt directly with prayer or which bore indirectly upon it. The first teaching which we must notice is, of course, the Lord's Prayer itself. It is the model for all Christian prayer and has certain aspects which any serious student of prayer ought to note carefully. A full examination of all its implications would be a big undertaking, and a treatise in itself. Our own immediate interest is limited to trying to see what the Lord's Prayer teaches us about the principles which our own prayer should adopt, and the approach which it should take.

For this purpose we will take the version of the prayer as it appears in the sixth chapter of St Matthew's Gospel, which in the New English Bible, differs from that in St Luke's. It is important to observe the first word "our" as meaning not only a prayer united with fellow Christians, but above all a prayer united with Christ and coming to the Father just because it is one with the prayer of Christ. This sets the tone of all Christian prayer, and marks it off sharply from any other Eastern form of mysticism which claims to approach God with no need of Jesus Christ. Though non-Christian prayer may have certain insights it cannot approach the fullness of the prayer of the Christian united with Christ in the Father—"as thou, Father, art in me, and I in thee, so also may they be in us" (John 17.21). It is important to stress this point as many commentators restrict their interpretation of the "our" of "Our Father" to the common prayer of Christians themselves. But the very appellation "Father" as well as the "our" can only be fully understood in the light of the revelation of Jesus Christ and our unity with him through his mystical Body, the Church, both in corporate and so-called "private" prayer.

The Lord's Prayer also teaches us the priority of prayer and what its character should be. It is not primarily petition, but primarily worship, submission to the will of God, recognition that God is heavenly, holy, the ruler of all. These concepts point to the inexhaustible riches of the truth about God, and also the direction to which true prayers should tend. It is not until these qualities of God have been recognized by the soul and have been—so to say—publicly admitted in his prayer, that there can be any meaning in the requests which a Christian makes to his heavenly Father. For without these preliminaries the requests are bound to be wrongly made.

It is part of the tragedy of many half-Christians to-day that they think the process can be reversed. They believe that it is their needs which come first and for which requests should first be made, and that God will be rewarded with their worship and admiration if he comes through the test.

We cannot examine the Lord's Prayer without referring to the difficulty of the phrase "lead us not into temptation". Most Christians probably take it as meaning "lead us not into more temptation than we can withstand", and this is a perfectly innocent gloss on the words, for, as they stand, their meaning is obscure. The general opinion among scholars seems to be that the "temptation" referred to is probably the great tribulation, to which there are various references in the Gospel, but that is to put a meaning on the word which it does not normally bear, either in English or in Greek.

If we are to take the word in its normal meaning without any addition or explanation, it is impossible to make proper sense of it, for it is obvious that all men are in fact going to be tempted or put to the test. (The New English Bible reads "and do not bring us to the test".) Indeed life itself is a form of testing, and to pray that we shall not be put to the test is equivalent to opting out of life altogether. Moreover, there is hardly any teacher in the spiritual life who does not clearly maintain that temptation or trial or test is an essential element in the progress of the spiritual life, and that without it there is no advancement.

The association of the last clauses of the prayer "and do not bring us to the test" and "but save us from the evil one" suggests another possible interpretation, namely that we are praying to be prevented from falling into the great temptation which our Lord himself faced in the wilderness, and to which he replied to the evil one, "Thou shalt not tempt the Lord thy God". To put God to the test is the ultimate blasphemy, and is a sin towards which the evil one is constantly trying to drive us.

The other two clauses of the prayer ask for our daily bread and for forgiveness, the basic necessities of physical and spiritual life. In the former case we ask only for what is needed and not for what is agreeable but unnecessary. We are not encouraged by Jesus to seek anything in our material life beyond what is needed for its proper upkeep.

As regards forgiveness, as all know, the phrase joins the forgiveness of God with our forgiveness of those who have wronged us. Without this forgiveness we cannot even *ask* forgiveness of of God, still less receive it. Jesus teaches us that this forgiveness of our neighbours is the absolute requirement in our own prayer for the forgiveness of God. The fact too that this clause is a permanent part of the prayer shows without doubt that the attitude of penitence and forgiveness on our part is to be a permanent element in our spiritual life. Forgiveness is not a static thing; it is the practical expression of an attitude of love, of our love for our neighbour and of God's love for us. It once more demonstrates in this practical way that love of God and love of our neighbour are not haphazardly brought together by God when he tells us the two great commandments of the law, but that one cannot exist without the other. We cannot love God without loving our neighbour, and any pretence that we can, merely shows our inability to understand the first things about the Gospel. As St John says (1 John 4.20), "But if a man says, 'I love God', while hating his brother, he is a liar. If he does not love the brother whom he has seen, it cannot be that he loves God whom he has not seen. And indeed this command comes to us from Christ himself: that he who loves God must also love his brother."

This truth is inescapably included in the Lord's Prayer when it speaks of forgiveness. But it should be noted in passing, as a practical point, that forgiving those who have wronged us does not mean feeling forgiving towards them, though we shall always do our best to encourage right emotional attitudes. It means, basically, acting in a forgiving way, showing in our actions the love which God has shed abroad in our own hearts, whatever passing feelings of resentment it may be necessary to disregard. Indeed, a forgiving act is more difficult, and in a certain way more praiseworthy (if any act is praiseworthy on the part of a human being), when feelings of dislike have to be overcome.

In general, therefore, we may say that the Lord's Prayer points us to the need for just those things which men of prayer have been seeking to find, above all else a greater realization in their own lives of the truth about God and a constant effort to submit their wills to his and to assimilate that will into their lives in every aspect. From the example of Jesus and from these principles we should naturally conclude that this can only be fully done when time is set apart for colloquy with God, and when the chief object of that time is to understand spiritually more and more the truth of God and to enter into spiritual contact with him.

We are not writing a treatise on how the New Testament approaches prayer, but we ought to notice that there are other passages besides those we have mentioned which bear on the subject. There are direct instructions on the subject, that personal prayer should not be made for everyone to see, that when it is made in the name of Jesus and in the company of two or three it will be granted, that persistence in prayer is necessary as in the case of the importunate widow, that God sees our needs before we ask and is anxious to meet them, that those with pure hearts shall see God, that some things can only be done through prayer, that humility in prayer is acceptable to God and self-satisfaction is not. Again and again we find sayings that point to the indispensability of prayer in the life of anyone who is trying to follow the will of God (e.g. Matt. 6.5f; 7.7; 17.21; 21.22; 26.41; Mark 9.29; 11.24f; 14.38; Luke 2.37; 11.9; 13.25; 18.1; 18.10; 22.40, 46).

All these extracts come out of one or other of the first three Gospels. When we come to the Gospel according to St John we find that prayer occupies an even more central place than in the other Gospels and that the Gospel itself is a sort of prayer, a form of meditation on the saving acts of Jesus Christ and their spiritual meaning for the world. In his Bampton Lectures for 1899 W. R. Inge said: "The Gospel of St John—the 'spiritual Gospel', as Clement already calls it—is the charter of Christian Mysticism. Indeed, Christian Mysticism, as I understand it, might almost be called Johannine Christianity; if it were not better to say that a Johannine Christianity is the ideal which the Christian mystic sets before himself."[1] Without at this point discussing the exact meaning of the phrase "Christian mysticism" we can certainly assert without fear of contradiction that the Gospel of St John is mainly concerned with the present relationship of the Christian with God through Christ, and that it speaks constantly of eternal life, not as some future reward for present actions, but as a possession to be had and developed here and now. This is the whole end of prayer, in whatever form it is practised, and this Gospel, therefore, drives every reader forward to plunge into the activity of prayer through which alone he can find growth in unity with God in Christ.

Perhaps the heart of St John's Gospel in the light of the prayer

[1] Op. cit., p. 44.

life is to be found in the prayer of Jesus contained in the seventeenth chapter. Here we find a passionate prayer for the spiritual unity of his followers with the Father and with himself. The unity is to be in some way comparable to the intimate union of the Father and the Son, the Christian being caught up in that unity through his prayer. It is difficult to imagine a more vivid way of expressing the aim of the spiritual life which is, evidently, the vocation of all the followers of Jesus. It is not a request that those who are specially gifted, or who may have more inclinations that way, should be brought to this unity of spirit, but all his disciples are included in the prayer.

In St Paul's letters we find constant instructions to continue in prayer, to pray without ceasing, for his readers to give themselves wholly to prayer, that they should let their requests be made known unto God. It is a theme which runs through his letters. In addition to this there are indications that St Paul had spiritual experiences of great intensity at the time of his vision on the Damascus road and afterwards during his ministry. We are not concerned with an analysis of what his theory of visions and other experiences was, but are merely trying to see how St Paul followed his Master in giving a prominent and important place to prayer in the life of those to whom he was guide and leader.

All this, one might say, is superfluous. It is not necessary to tell people that the New Testament is in favour of prayer, since everyone knows it already. There are two points to be made in reply to such an objection. The first is that there are those who maintain that the life of prayer is an alien introduction into Christianity from elsewhere and is no part of the original Gospel. Now while it is true that in Christian history there are to be found theories of prayer, and in some cases methods of prayer which do not accord with the teaching of the New Testament, yet these are aberrations and do not affect the main stream. Without trying here to discuss what is an aberration and what is not, it is enough to say that in the New Testament there can be no possible doubt that the practice of prayer by individual persons is meant to be an indispensable part of their religious life.

The second point is the undoubted fact that vast numbers of

people who consider themselves Christians, and even go regularly to their churches, do not in fact practise prayer in their daily lives. They do not see it as so important that time has to be made for it. Were they more convinced that the life of prayer is an essential element of the Christian life in the New Testament they would perhaps be more ready to make the effort which is always required to ensure that prayer has a permanent place in their daily lives, and to pursue it not on the model of an inadequate prayer learnt at their mothers' knees, but in the fullness of Christian growth as revealed in Jesus Christ himself, both in his life and his teaching.

9

Liturgy and Prayer

Of the many words which have been wrongly used to the great confusion of thought, "individual" and "personal" must rank high. As they are often needed in religious discussion much damage has been done by this wrong use. For the Christian there is no such thing as an individual in the strict sense. Man does not, cannot, and will not ever exist out of relation to his fellow men and to God, and therefore to consider him as an individual in the religious sphere is to pretend that he is something other than he is. False premises lead to false conclusions. Man is a person, and the word "person" includes in its meaning a man's relationship to others. The word "individual" has the effect of making one think of persons as entirely separate from one another, and needs to be carefully watched.

The Church has always stressed the truth of the dependence of men on one another, both within her fold and outside it. The doctrine of original sin enshrines the latter truth, since it teaches that every human being is contaminated by the sinfulness of the world by reason of his birth alone, for he shares in the common sinfulness of his own stock. There are some signs of a return to this basic belief, which has been out of fashion in various quarters, and which is so clearly taught in the first chapters of the book of Genesis; no interpretation of human facts and needs which leaves it out of account can meet the requirements of truth.

To find similar teaching within the Christian Church we need only take one example from the New Testament—St Paul's teaching about the Body of Christ. As A. M. Ramsey pointed out:

The word σῶμα (body) in pre-Christian Greek, whether classical or biblical or hellenistic, did not mean a "body" of people or a society, in the manner of the English use of the word "body" or the Latin use of "corpus" as a social metaphor. . . . It did not suggest a group of persons. Hence to call the Church τὸ σῶμα τοῦ χριστοῦ was to draw attention to it not primarily as a collection of men, but primarily as Christ Himself in His own being and life.[1]

The Church is Christ's body, the Christians are the members or limbs (τὰ μέλη), and Christ is the head (ἡ κεφαλή). It would be difficult to find a more powerful analogy than this to express the way in which Christians are bound together—to each other and to Christ. No analogy must be pressed too far, but the point here is that St Paul sees Christ and all the members of the Church as forming one indivisible unity, one living organism, and not simply an organization. Many other examples of this teaching could be given, both from the New Testament and from the Fathers; our Lord's metaphor "I am the vine; ye are the branches" emphasizes precisely the same truth.

In any discussion about prayer this background must constantly be kept in mind. When we consider the prayer life of different Christians, it is necessary theoretically to separate Christians from one another and to treat them as individual persons, but this is an abstraction for a special object, namely, to find the proper course of action for any one person. But prayer can no more be considered as essentially individual than can any other part of the Christian life. In the Church no action of any one member is private, except in the sense that it may be unknown to others. Every action by every Christian affects the Church as a whole for good or ill. A sin weakens the sinner, and therefore the whole church is weakened, and contrariwise an act of faithfulness strengthens the whole Church. So prayer—however private in being unknown to other human beings—is an act affecting the whole Church.

But this is not all. Superficially prayer may appear to be independent of others, but in fact prayer is only made in the Church and through the Church. We can only approach God in Christian prayer because we are members of Christ, baptized into his Body and therefore part of him. We cannot come to God in prayer in

[1] *The Gospel and The Catholic Church*, p. 35.

any full sense by virtue of being his children by creation. Could we do so, the Incarnation of Jesus Christ would be unnecessary and we should be at liberty to use him as an optional means of reaching God. But "there is none other name under heaven given among men whereby we must be saved" (Acts 4.2). This is the clear Gospel of the New Testament and of the Church. The words "he that believeth and is baptized shall be saved" (Mark 16.16) supplies the other emphasis, equally strong, that there is no way of following our Lord in completeness except by being born again into his Body, the Church.

This is the context in which Christians have prayed throughout history. This is the background which must be assumed in any examination of prayer, even when these facts are not explicitly mentioned. We do not approach God by any right of our own, but only by the right belonging to us as members of Christ, the children of God, and inheritors of the kingdom of heaven by baptism.

The private prayers of Christians, therefore, are not to be regarded as exercises of individual spirits, but as contributions made to the total act of worship offered continually by the whole Church. Such prayers are part of the Church's liturgy. Just as the Church acts in the Eucharist through a particular priest and congregation as her representatives, offering the one eternal sacrifice of the cross, so in private acts of devotion the Church is acting through a particular Christian person. The priesthood of the laity is more than a pious phrase for the edification of those who hear sermons; it includes the same kind of responsibility as is basic in the sacred Ministry, the authority of the Church herself. Lutherans are quite right when they stress the importance of the priesthood of the laity, and say that there is a universal priesthood, though not a universal Ministry. But this does not mean that the laity have no ministry, but only that they have not the particular Ministry of Bishops, Priests, and Deacons. The laity have a ministry of great importance. Their part in the celebration of the Eucharist is indispensable, but it is a mistake to assume that the worship of the Church as a whole is confined to public worship in church—that is merely the centre. This worship is to be found in the lives of the laity in all their details including their lives of prayer. Every prayer offered in private by a Christian adds to the worship given by the Church to God. None of this activity can be replaced by public services in churches.

It is right that the part to be played in the Church by the laity should be stressed, but too often this part is pictured as necessary merely for practical reasons. There is nothing false in the statement that in the conversion of the world it is the lay men and women who must carry the message of the Gospel to their fellow men. If, however, that is all that laymen hear, they will lack the inspiration to do the work. There is need that lay people should be taught more of the essential character of their co-operation in the worship of the Church, and of what that worship consists.

Although the Eucharist alone cannot replace the worship of the Church in the private lives of her members, it is in the Eucharist that all private prayer must be focused, inspired, and expressed. No prayer life can possibly be full that omits or discounts the first importance of the corporate worship of the Eucharist. Here is prayer in its perfection, a perfection which is independent of the attention or devotion of any particular congregation. We do not say, therefore, that the devotion of the congregation is of no account, but the Eucharist has a perfection which is not affected by the congregation or the priest, because it is conferred by our Lord himself. In every Eucharist there is set forth the offering of Christ himself, in every Eucharist there is the Body broken and the Blood shed. Here is the ideal of prayer constantly shown in the sacrifice of Jesus on the cross. The root of all true prayer is submission to the will of God, and the chief service of the Body of Christ eternally presents to God before the world that sacrifice in which conformity to God's will is perfectly shown.

As we have seen elsewhere, this expresses the root of all true prayer—conformity to the will of God. Descriptions of prayer as "conversation with God" or "the uplifting of the soul to God" are only partially accurate and may even be misleading. "Religion is adoration" wrote Baron von Hügel; that is why prayer is at the centre of religion. In prayer Christians begin to take part in the activity for which they were created and redeemed, the adoration of God. Those who are saved and raised to heaven are occupied in the praise and adoration of God. "These are they which came out of great tribulation, and have washed their robes, and made them white in the blood of the Lamb. Therefore are they before the throne and serve him day and night in his temple." (Rev. 7.14.)

In adoration alone is to be found the complete fulfilment of man's spiritual nature. Through the submission of the will to the Holy Spirit of God the spirit of adoration may be received from him.

The Eucharist is the fount whence flows the spirit of adoration to the Church and its members. This sacrament is the means of grace for the lives of men, and especially for that part of their lives which is concerned with the exercise of their spiritual faculties. Prayer must receive its impress from Christ's own service, and at the altar must receive the strength given by God through the Holy Spirit. The Church's worship in the Eucharist supplies that balance in spiritual things which is needed to avoid the dangers of self-centredness.

Private prayer, then, is an essential part of the liturgy of the Church in its widest sense. It both contributes to and draws from the spiritual life of the Body. It gives its own self to the whole, and in turn receives first the strength and the grace of God, and second, a right relationship to God, to the Church, and to other Christians.

10

A Life for Every Man

When "mystical experience" was mentioned to a man who had spent all his life dealing with Church affairs, he replied that he did not understand what it was, and that he considered it only something mysterious. It is a great misfortune that the mystical life has become an affair for specialists, even in Christendom. In the East this would cause no surprise for it is avowedly a practice for the élite, a kind of spiritual gnosticism, only open to those specially trained to know it.

Sir Richard Tute wrote, "what really singles out the Christian religion from all other religions is the fact that whereas the medicine man and the Yogi regard their spiritual perception as a mark of spiritual superiority, the Christian religion proceeds on a diametrically opposite principle".[1] He goes on to stress the universality of the Christian message, and in doing so, follows a great series of Christian teachers and men of prayer.

"God does not reserve such a lofty vocation [mystical contemplation] to certain souls only; on the contrary, He is willing that all should embrace it. But he finds few who permit Him to work such sublime things for them."[2] St Catherine of Genoa teaches the same thing: "And man, every man, is capable of this pure love and of the truth which such love sees. 'I see every one to be capable of my tender love.'"[3] Dozens of other witnesses could be called to the stand.

Whether we accept Sir Richard Tute's remarks exactly as they stand or not, there should be no hesitation in agreeing that

[1] *After Materialism What?*, p. 195 n.
[2] St John of the Cross, quoted by Aldous Huxley in *The Perennial Philosophy*, p. 340.
[3] Quoted by von Hügel in *Mystical Element of Religion*, vol. i, p. 268.

in Christianity the mystical life ought to be something in which every Christian takes part, and of which every Christian knows the elements. But it is unhappily not so.

In modern times all life is departmentalized to an extent which has disastrous results on the wholeness of living which men need. Thus scientists are apt to think that their labours are the be-all and end-all of existence, and some of them even go so far as to deny the validity of other disciplines such as theology and philosophy. In a similar vein business men have invented the saying "business is business", and the artists "art for art's sake", while psychological determinism has seduced some of the psychologists.

All these signs are symptoms of the same disease, a failure to see life in its completeness and to relate one branch of life to another. To this disease writers on mysticism have contributed, though the offenders have been not so much the mystics themselves as their well-meaning supporters. The mystical life has been presented as an affair for specialists and not for the ordinary man, and it has become departmentalized within religion.

Some blame for this must rest on the medieval conception of the double standard. In the crude conditions where this idea first grew up it may be explained, though from a Christian point of view it can never be justified. In short the double standard is the belief that there are two standards, one for those who take their religion seriously as a whole-time job, and the other for those who are busy earning their livings or fulfilling other duties and who can only give a certain amount of time to it. Monks and nuns were on one side of the line and ordinary workaday people on the other.

The whole assumption of such an attitude is false, since, if Christianity does not affect the whole of every Christian's life, it is useless and has no message worth hearing. Certainly some men may be called to give their lives as monks to the service of God, but their vocation is no "higher" than the man who gives his life as a father, or a worker, or a scientist, or an artist. The "highest" vocation for each man is that to which God calls him. If he is called to be a Christian mechanic, he would be following a lower path if he became a monk. If a woman is called to be a mother, that is her highest vocation, for the simple reason that it is God's will for her. If the vocation of monks and nuns were "higher", all who did not become monks or nuns would in some measure be falling short of God's will. Yet the false conception still exists, and is perhaps encouraged by the fact that the monastic life is still called "the religious life" and those who follow it are known as "Religious", suggesting that others are not.

It is partly this misleading tradition which has caused the mystical life to become a specialized affair, since it became natural to think that it was the special provenance of monastic Christians, or of others who had plenty of time, such as widows, or ladies of leisure. Of course members of the monastic orders have special opportunities for concentrating on the life of prayer, for their rule is aimed at making it easier for them to do so. It is clearly simpler for a monk in a well-run monastery to pray regularly and for a fixed time than it is for a mother who has a young family with first claim on her attention and care.

This, however, does not mean that the opportunities for Christian development are greater for the monk. It may be quite the other way round. While he is labouring with spiritual difficulties, the mother, by making a whole offering of her maternal duties to God, and by receiving the love of God into her life, may advance much further much quicker than the monk.

Spiritual development and mystical development are the same thing. The mystical life cannot and must not be restricted to the kind of experiences which are recorded in the books of those who have advanced far along the road of concentrated prayer. Such books are important as spiritual classics, providing an immense amount of information and instruction in the spiritual life. But they are only one part of an immensely rich and varied mystical life in the Church as a whole.

The mystical life varies as much as life itself and as much as the people living it vary. The mystical life is as broad as mankind, and each man will have an experience which differs in some respect from that of every other person. For the experience will depend on several variable factors. First on what God thinks to be best for each person; second, on what are that person's inherent capacities; third, on what stage the person has reached; fourth, on what are his outward circumstances of life.

It is possible, of course, to concentrate one's study on what we may loosely call the great mystics. But the dangers of this are so great as to need careful guards against them. They should be studied only to derive from them certain principles common to all Christian spiritual life, and these should be rigidly distinguished so far as possible from those elements which are likely to be peculiar to the mystic in question.

Attention must also be drawn to the fact that the Christian mystics differ among themselves on certain very important practical points. Where they differ the reader must fall back on those theological principles which must ever remain his guide, and from them derive his judgement as to which is the right road.

Those who set out to describe spiritual experiences are always faced with a preliminary difficulty from which they can never escape. How is it possible to put into language the deepest of their experiences? "What [divine men] hold to be true is raised above all images and forms, in a pure feeling of the divine good, of which no one can speak . . . they do not give to be understood what they know, and cannot at all express it in words."[1] And J. H. Newman wrote: "The pure and indivisible light is seen only by the blessed inhabitants of heaven; here we have but such faint reflections of it as its diffraction supplies; but they are sufficient for faith and devotion. Attempt to combine them into one, and you gain nothing but a mystery, which you can describe as a notion, but cannot depict as an imagination."[2]

Human language was invented to describe material things and from this it was extended for certain abstract purposes. Neither of these uses is of much help in describing spiritual experiences. When, therefore, we read the mystics we do not read their spiritual experiences but an interpretation or approximation to them in human language. We are then already one stage away from them, and the greatest care must be exercised in not pressing

[1] J. Tauler, *The Following of Christ*, vol. ii, ch. 46.
[2] Quoted in *The Spear of Gold*, p. 20.

too far the actual words and expressions in which they clothe their tale.

But the mystical vocation is basically the same for all, even though the experiences are different. And although they are different they belong to the same family of experiences, namely experience of true life, the life which Christ came to bring to men, eternal life. "Of all the doctrine which our Blessed Lord delivered in so many and such divine discourses this was the sum— that man should absolutely and entirely conform himself to the will of God . . . the measure of our spiritual growth lies entirely in the conformity and agreement of the human will with the Divine, so that in proportion as the one is genuine, the other will be luxuriant."[1]

[1] Drexelius, *The Heliotropium*, 1st para.

11

Authenticity

It is natural in writing about the prayer life or mysticism to inquire what it is that authenticates any mystical experience: how do we know that it is of value? (The term "mystical experience" is used in a wide sense to include spiritual experiences of various kinds associated with the activity of prayer and religious living.) Yet such an inquiry is so often omitted from writings on the subject that it is a rarity. Christianity is not the only religion which contains examples of this kind of experience. The religions of the East contain highly developed systems of spiritual training, which in some ways receive more emphasis there than they do within Christianity.

A Christian ought, therefore, to have some idea as to whether he thinks Eastern mysticism to be as authentic as Christian mysticism or not. And if not, he should be able to give some reason for his view. For whatever may be said to the detriment of the spiritual exercises of the East, there is no doubt that they give remarkable results in the physical sphere and in the control which is exercised by adepts over their bodily actions. It is impossible for a detached observer to deny the reality of Eastern spirituality, or the fact that its effects outwardly are impressive.

There are many different kinds of mystical experience, varying both according to different religions and according to differences in personal make-up and ability. Adherents of different systems have much in common with one another. As Dean Inge wrote: "You may take up mystical books written in Europe, Asia and America; two thousand years ago and last year; by men and women; by Catholics and Protestants; by philosophers and

93

unlearned, ignorant people; and if they were all translated into modern English, you would hardly be able to distinguish them."[1] But although the common element is not to be minimized, it must be recognized that there are equally important matters on which mystics differ, and it is here that the problem arises. If all those with mystical experience agreed on everything, it might be possible to maintain that their words had to be accepted. It can still be claimed that where their experiences are common, they are substantially reliable, but even when this is agreed, there is a wide field where other standards must be applied to make a judgement.

It is, therefore, impossible to regard all mystical experience as self-authenticating. The various strands must be judged by outside measuring rods. How is it possible to evaluate the experience of a Yogi as compared with a Christian saint? This can surely only be done by the application of the normal standards of philosophy and theology. The mystical life is not something which is independent of normal reason and revelation, even though in some ways it goes beyond reason. It must submit itself to the same canons as religion in general.

In short we may say that while the mystical experience is real and objective, both its expression and its interpretation are subjective and will reflect the intellectual shortcomings and even errors of the subject. Mystical experience is, it is true, to be judged by results. "By their fruits ye shall know them." But the fruits to be looked for must be discovered by theology in its widest sense. To put the matter plainly, a mystical experience is to be judged not by the ability of the subject to bury himself in the sand for three weeks and remain alive, but by whether it produces the fruits of love and humility; not, that is, by apparent miracle, but by moral growth according to the standards of Christian love.

It is one of the tragic elements of Christianity that miracle and sanctity have been mixed so closely together, and that the Roman Church continues to encourage it. Miracles never have been and can never be a proof of sanctity in a Christian society. (The word

[1] *Speculum Animae*, pp. 5f.

"miracle" is used in its popular sense to mean any inexplicable event which appears to be beyond a "natural" explanation. The question of the proper use of the word is outside the present inquiry.) From a Christian point of view the only relevance of a miracle must lie in its moral content. This is the teaching of the New Testament and the attitude of Jesus Christ. He refused to do certain miracles (in the story of the temptations, for example) because they would have made the wrong impression on those to whom he brought his message. If miracle *per se* is to be taken as indicating sanctity, Christianity will have some difficult problems in the East.

Miracle, in the sense in which we are using the word, only indicates power, if it is considered apart from its moral content. The physical effects which are shown to follow from spiritual power simply witness to its effectiveness, which may itself be either desirable or undesirable. The Christian mystics are agreed on this point, though not in the same words. Their attitude to supernatural phenomena in general is conclusive. All the mystics agree that no trust of any kind is to be put in supernatural experiences whether spiritual, quasi-material, or physical. In themselves such experiences may be evil, good, or indifferent. Christianity has always maintained a belief in the existence of evil as well as of good spirits.

To support these statements perhaps the following quotation from St John of the Cross may suffice:

Some spiritual persons persuade themselves—not reflecting on the great curiosity which they often display when they seek knowledge from God in supernatural ways—because their prayers are sometimes answered, that their conduct in the matter is good and pleasing unto God. Nevertheless the truth is notwithstanding the answers they receive, that God is offended and not pleased. And more than this, they provoke Him to anger, and displease Him greatly. The reason is this—no creature may transgress the limits which God hath appointed in the order of its being for its rule and guidance. He has ordained for man's governance certain natural and reasonable laws, the transgression of which is therefore not right; now, to seek anything by supernatural ways is to transgress these laws, and therefore an unholy and unbecoming thing, and displeasing unto God.[1]

The New Testament teaches that it is the undiscerning who are interested in miracles as such, those who do not see the point of the message. So Jesus said: "This is an evil generation; they seek a sign; and there shall no sign be given it, but the sign of Jonas the prophet." (Luke 11.29.) The interest in miracles indicates a desire to judge Christianity by the wrong results. The Christian religion does produce results, but they are results in the characters of men and women. Other results are secondary in the sense that they depend on these changes in men's characters.

The mystical life cannot, therefore, be judged by the phenomena of an extraordinary kind in the material world. No one would deny that there is a connection between spiritual power and strange physical occurrences, least of all those who know personally either primitive religions such as those in Africa, or the highly developed religions of the East. But more is needed for moral judgement, and to decide what is good and what is not one must fall back on other principles.

The Christian mystical writers acknowledge this in making, as they often do, their writings subject to the judgement of the Church. This is the natural safeguard for them, and a proper one. What the judgement of the Church is and how it is expressed poses other questions. The standard theological test must be the teaching of the New Testament and its development in the history of Christian piety accepted as authentic by the general consensus of the Church.

Those Christians who refer not to some all-knowing and all-reliable authority but to the New Testament must face many problems, which do not weigh upon their brethren who have an unquestionable authority for their instruction. But a sense of responsibility for wrestling with such problems is a necessary element in the development of the fullness of Christian character, and will not be evaded by those who consider spiritual and personal liberty one of the basic motifs of the Gospel of Christ.

[1] *Ascent of Mount Carmel*, bk ii, ch. 21.

A fourteenth-century mystic wrote: "For the truth is revealed and disclosed in the Holy Scripture, and therefore it is not needful that the truth should be revealed to us in another way. And whoso taketh truth otherwise than out of the Gospel he is sick in faith, and not much is to be thought of his life, for our life is only from the Gospel."[1]

[1] J. Tauler, *The Following of Christ*, vol. ii, ch. 27.

12

Penitence

The Christian view of sin and of penitence is often widely distorted by the introduction into it of a legalistic outlook. Christian people are inclined to think too much of sins and too little of sin, causing themselves to become preoccupied with acts of sin. This approach may obscure the real importance of sin as a destruction of the right relation between God and man.

The reason for this false emphasis must certainly be found far back in Christian history. The impression given by Dr Telfer's study of the history of Christian doctrine and practice[1] is that even in the early Church, where the impact of our Lord's personal teaching would be expected to be strongest, an essentially legalistic view was predominant. It is ironic that this should have been the case, since it is evident in the New Testament that the whole context of the forgiveness of sins is the restoration of right relationship with God. Dr Telfer points out that the context of the forgiveness of sins in the New Testament and early Church was eschatological, it took place in the atmosphere and hope of the triumph of God in the last things, which was shortly expected to occur. "Accordingly sins are not treated as so many incidents, but as all rooted in a power of evil with which God will make an end."[2]

It is sometimes assumed that although the early Christians were expecting the end of the world in the near future, this expectation did not lead them astray in their attitudes. But in the case we are considering their beliefs about sins after baptism were directly affected by their over-riding conviction that it would be only a *short* time before their Master returned in triumph and his

[1] *The Forgiveness of Sins.*   [2] Ibid., p. 19.

rule was completely vindicated. The result of this wrong conviction was that they thought themselves able to live at a level which they would not have considered possible had they envisaged a future of centuries to come.

Dr Telfer asks: "Was it expected, then, of those who received this eschatological forgiveness, that they would thereafter cease from sin?"[1] and continues: "The answer which the earliest Christian writings seem to testify is in the affirmative." We have here an example of wrong thinking which much affected the early Church and many developments throughout Christian history, namely the confusion between living in a state of forgiveness with God and the cessation of acts of sin. The two are different problems and must be carefully distinguished.

But first a warning must be sounded. It is not suggested that the forgiveness of God which comes to man has no connection with actual sinning, still less that one who has received such forgiveness has a licence to continue committing sins. Such an idea would be absurd. But the experience of forgiveness does not and should not be expected to mean that no further sins are ever committed again. Sins are a permanent part of human life in its fallen state, and their relative seriousness varies almost infinitely with the personality and the circumstances of those who commit them.

Luther has emphasized this truth with his phrase *simul justus et peccator*—"at one and the same time justified and a sinner". This phrase points to the important truth that the sting of sin is that it breaks the fellowship which ought to exist between God and man. "The 'paradoxical' character of forgiveness is expressed in the fact that divine love, which stands in unabridged opposition to sin, receives sinful man into its fellowship."[2] The stress which Lutherans give to this aspect of forgiveness brings out a truth which has been sadly obscured by the attitudes of other exponents of Western theology, especially by the moral theology of the Roman and Anglican Churches. Much of the attention in such studies has been concentrated on acts of sin, isolated from other considerations, thus encouraging the idea that this is the correct way to deal with questions of sin.

[1] Ibid.   [2] Gustaf Aulén, *The Faith of the Christian Church*, p. 289.

The Church early promoted a legalistic approach to sin by categorizing it into major and minor sins, and by holding that there was an unforgiveable sin after baptism. Such a point of view had in time to be modified, but its main fault was the introduction into Christian thinking of the idea that sins were in themselves to be considered without relating them to the question of the sinner's spiritual attitude or condition.

No doubt a legalistic approach was encouraged by the primitive beliefs of the time about the human personality. Modern knowledge has greatly increased our understanding of the content of the human personality, and of the elements which affect moral responsibility in the behaviour of men and women. Indeed there is some tendency to reduce the area of moral responsibility to so small a point that it is difficult to use the word "responsibility" at all. This is going too far. But to an age which had no idea of these facts about personality, sins were often far too easily ascribed to independent acts of the will, when they might just as easily have been the outcome of uncontrollable emotional disorder.

The over-simplified terms in which early Christians thought also tended to make them think of moral actions as direct evidence either of loyalty to Christ, or conversely of possession by evil powers. Those who sinned after baptism could, therefore, be thought to have sold themselves to the devil or to be possessed by some evil spirit, and they would, therefore, naturally be assumed to have put themselves outside the Christian fold.

There was, of course, need for discipline in the early Church, as also in later times. The question of the "public image" of the Church—to use a modern phrase—had to be considered, and causes of grave scandal had to be removed. We do not suggest that the problem was a simple one, and St Paul was no doubt right in ruling that those who insist on defying the principles of the Faith ought to be cast out (1 Cor. 5.5). Sometimes action has to be taken for the sake of the body as a whole which would not be desirable if the interests of the individual alone were to be considered. These are matters which cannot be ignored by those responsible for the conduct of Church affairs.

But the need for some action does not change the basic misfortune that Christian thought about penitence and forgiveness came to be largely concentrated on sins instead of on the state of sinfulness, and that even to-day the wrong emphasis persists in men's minds. Corruptions against which the Lutheran Reformation protested were often bound up with a legalistic approach, for example in the sale of indulgences and in the beliefs about sin and punishment of which that was one manifestation. Yet the Christians of the reformed Churches themselves did not remain free of the mistake for long and are not noticeably more free from it than other Christians now.

The greatest danger of putting too much emphasis on sins is that it leads to the idea that God's forgiveness is in some way measured by the achievements of him who is to be forgiven. Dr H. R. Mackintosh puts the point:

> Surely there is less presumption in taking my complete forgiveness from God's hand at the outset and always later, as a purely living gift, than in coming to Him afterwards, at intervals, with the sense that I am now a better man and therefore fitter to be forgiven. Nothing more apt than this to breed self-consciousness could be imagined. The truth is, when securities for a good life are demanded from the sinful before forgiveness full and free is placed in their hand, the result is to turn Christianity into a form of morality rather than a religion.[1]

It is clear that we must avoid any idea that sins do not matter. Indeed the more we are aware of the forgiveness which God has freely bestowed on us, the more serious we see sins to be. There is, as so often in the Christian life, a tension which has to be maintained, a balance which must not be upset, between the avoidance of sins on the one hand and the understanding that sins can only be seen in their right meaning when viewed, not in themselves as moral acts, but in their significance as the expression of the personality and its relation to the living God.

What matters most of all—indeed it alone matters—is the spiritual connection between God and the person. It is a person who is the subject of the love of God and the aim of the redeeming acts of Jesus Christ. God does not promise freedom from sins in

[1] *The Christian Experience of Forgiveness*, p. 243.

this life, but he promises a way of breaking through the barrier which sin sets up between the soul and God, a way of finding and receiving the love of God in spite of the sins which stain and twist the personality. It is, therefore, important to understand rightly what is the character of Christian penitence and of God's forgiveness.

Penitence is best described as we have said, by the original Greek word of which it is a translation—*metanoia*—a change of mind, indicating a new direction deliberately taken by the spirit towards God. It is in this redirection that penitence essentially consists—in other words it is a permanent attitude or state of mind, and not something which only exists in relation to particular sins. Its basic character is not sorrow, or contrition, or attrition, or anything else in relation to particular acts of sin: these are tests of penitence, not its constituent parts. Acts of sin may be, and very often are, the occasions for penitence or expressions of penitence. But penitence itself is an underlying attitude of the spirit.

This underlying attitude of the spirit is the act of faith or will, by which we cling to God, or look towards him, with confidence in his love to us. It includes the realization of our own unworthiness, sinfulness, failures, of all our human weaknesses, and at the same time has a glimpse of the holiness of God as well as of his all-powerful love. Penitence, therefore, is not something which comes and goes according to whether we can find some sins or not, it is rather a permanent part of the truly Christian spirit. Without it there can be no fellowship with God at all, for it is the indispensable preliminary to coming to him in faith and love.

This truth has the important corollary, which is evident to all theologians but widely misunderstood by everyday Christians, that God loves us as we are and does not demand some achievements as the price of earning his love. God speaks to the soul in such words as these: "Offer yourself to me as you are. Do not wait to be satisfied with yourself. Unite yourself to me in your worst poverty. I take you, I redeem you, if you trust me to do it. Have faith. Who is there who loves you more than I?"[1] A sense

[1] Gabrielle Bossis, *LUI et Moi. Entretiens spirituels*, vol vii, no. 174. (7 volumes. Beauchesne, Paris.)

of unworthiness, which is so essential to the receiving of the gift of forgiveness, can by a curious inversion become the very means of preventing people from coming to find it. If the emphasis is legalistic, then the sense of unworthiness is a barrier to God just because the person knows himself to be incapable of achieving the level of righteousness which would justify him in approaching God or "earning" forgiveness. It is appalling how widely this inverted doctrine of merit has spread in Christendom. The Roman Church has some remedy for it in the sacrament of Confession, as have the Orthodox and Anglicans, and in the Protestant Churches the remedy should be found through the right preaching of the Word. But only too often both methods fail to rid their people of this twisted approach.

What then is forgiveness? The popular idea is often that it is God kindly agreeing to overlook acts of sin which have annoyed him. God is anthropomorphically likened to a kind old gentleman. It is needless to say that such ideas cloak the reality of God's love and turn it into a kind of humanitarian benevolence. Forgiveness is simply the active love of God reaching out to rescue the sinner from his selfishness and sin and helping him to turn again towards God. Sin is the turning away from God, the rejection of him who is the soul's only health and salvation. It is the attitude of mind which installs self in the place of God in the spiritual life, and thus ensures misery and frustration in this life and in the world to come. Forgiveness is God reaching to the sinner through and in spite of his barrier of sin and making that personal contact with him which is the stuff of the spiritual life.

Penitence is the response to this love and is, therefore, a permanent part of the Christian life here on earth. We do not get to a time when penitence is no longer necessary here on earth because we are continually conscious of our own shortcomings in relation to God. We know that even when we are not consciously committing acts of sin our failures, now unwilling failures, are for the most part the result of turning away from God in the past. The results of our sin remain with us as scars, or deformities, for all our earthly life. And so the great saints still have an attitude of penitence at the bottom of their spiritual life, and the more they come close to God the more acute is their sense of their own unworthiness and shortcomings. Thus St Francis of Assisi calmly accepted ill-treatment and abuse from the porter who took him for a vagabond, saying that "the porter recognizes us for what we are".[1]

Dr Aulén points out[2] that there is a danger that the idea of forgiveness may be interpreted merely as a remission of a penalty due to sin. This is a reversion to the same legalistic approach which we have seen to be so damaging in thinking of sin. Most human analogies, whether that of a human law court or of a family, can encourage such wrong thought. But the truest human father of a family can also help to point us to the true conception, used in the same way in which Jesus himself spoke of God as Father. A true father, perhaps a mother even more, loves his children as they are: forgiveness is the re-establishment of a broken relationship, not the absence of punishment for an offence: and so it is with God.

In the understanding of the spiritual life from its most elementary beginnings until its flowering in the saints, hardly anything can be so destructive as the introduction of legal categories into this relationship between God and the soul. If the relationship is understood aright, moreover, the seriousness of acts of sin becomes heightened rather than lowered. No one who has ever grasped the reality of forgiveness can pretend to himself or others that sins do not matter; on the other hand he will not despair because he finds himself falling into sin, rather he will get up after his fall and stumble on in the direction in which he knows God to be. We shall not sin that grace may abound, but in our sins we shall find the power of God's love to raise us up again and again.

Part of the activity of God's forgiveness through repentance is that he exorcizes the evil spirits within us—if we may use the phrase. Our sins are the outcome not only of our free acts of will, but of all that lies beneath the level of full consciousness. While we cannot ever say that we are not responsible for our sins, we

---

[1] *Little Flowers of St Francis*, VII.   [2] Op. cit., p. 291.

can recognize there are underlying emotions and twists within us which reduce our moral responsibility in some instances, though without abolishing it, unless we are suffering from some pathological condition. A legalistic view of sin and forgiveness prevents us from allowing the healing influence of God's love to enter the depths of our spiritual and emotional life and to work its healing there.

For these reasons the traditional distinction between mortal and venial sins should be abandoned. The first bad effect which it has is to suggest that there are some sins which matter and some which do not. No amount of explanation can prevent this notion from spreading, especially when it is supported by rules, such as those in the Roman Church, which require confession only in the case of mortal sins. It is obvious to all that sins differ in gravity, both objectively and subjectively, or to use the phrase of the moral theologian, both materially and formally. It is important that those who have pastoral responsibilities should be able to distinguish between the gravity of sins and have training in doing so. But for the ordinary Christian this is not necessary, except in the broadest terms.

The second reason against maintaining the distinction between mortal and venial sins is that it is unreal, and has ceased to be useful in making clear distinctions, especially since modern psychology has revealed something of the power of the unconscious. It is in fact in many cases impossible to decide whether a sin is mortal, according to the traditional categories, without a prolonged examination by a psychiatrist. It is certainly quite impossible for a priest hearing confessions to do so without considerably more knowledge than confession would provide. People have guilt feelings which are out of proportion to their real condition. As a consequence the subjective tests which are traditionally applied to discover whether a sin is mortal or not, namely that the sinner must be fully aware of the evil character and consequences of the sin, and that in spite of this he must have sinned with absolute deliberateness and intention, have come to be impossible to apply.

These seem to be the inevitable conclusions of a study by Fr

Gérard Gilleman, s.j.,[1] although he does not express them in quite so bald a fashion. Yet the abandonment of the traditional methods of dealing with the subject must be the inevitable consequence of accepting the principles which he rightly puts forward:

> Christian life is defined much more profoundly by fidelity to charity-love than by the observance of law. Moral obedience to law is rather the exterior aspect, the necessary mediation of our profound life which is love, so that moral life can be defined only by reference to charity. . . . As an immoral act, sin is a transgression of the law, but this transgression is only the moral and exterior aspect of an actual disorder in our power of loving.[2]

He quotes St Thomas Aquinas as defining sin as *appetitio deordinata*, and throughout his book claims to be truly interpreting the Scholastic master. But even this term introduces too much the category of order rather than of personal relations which is the true centre of the matter, as he himself recognizes, though he does so without drawing what would seem to be the necessary radical conclusions.[3]

The trouble with the Latin tradition is that it is too firmly wedded to a method of categorization, of putting everything tidily in packets and pigeon holes, and over-defining mysterious things which only become impoverished by such definition. This has been and is the bane of Roman moral theology, from which Fr Gilleman's book is an effort to escape by introducing the all-pervading and all-embracing concept of love. That it should have been necessary or even possible for him to write such a book is itself a witness to the fact that the accepted treatment had lost its hold on some basic truths.

The important fact to grasp is that sins do not necessarily break our relationship with God, but that sin does. And sin does so because it is by definition a turning away from God by the free act of the human will, and God will not force himself on those who do not freely seek him or respond to his love. Julian of Norwich realized this and expressed it:

[1] *The Primacy of Charity in Moral Theology.*
[2] Op. cit., p. 279.   [3] Ibid., p. 280.

Although our Lord shewed me that I should sin, by me alone I understood all men. At this I conceived a soft dread, and to this our Lord answered me thus: "I keep thee full surely". This word was said to me with more love and sureness of ghostly keeping than I can or may tell. For, as it was before shewed to me that I should sin, right so was the comfort shewed to me: sureness of keeping for all my fellow-Christians.[1]

"Scripture, Faith and Truth say: Sin is nought else, but that the creature turns away from the unchangeable Good and betakes itself to the changeable; that is to say, that it turns away from the Perfect to that which is in part and imperfect, and most often to itself." That is how the second chapter of *Theologia Germanica* begins.[2] It is not necessary to look very far in the spiritual writers of the Middle Ages to find the truth there too: it is the ecclesiastics and canon lawyers who have taken the life out of the doctrine and made it mere regulations.

An objection may then be raised that, in spite of our earlier disclaimer, the effect of this approach is to introduce laxity and to make men careless of sins, so that they feel that it does not much matter whether they commit them or not. To this the answer must be, first, that if a man has once known something of what the forgiveness of sin really is, something of the love of God in action in his own life, he cannot regard acts of sin lightly while he still has the desire to come to God and to do his will. In the second place, if he has lost this understanding and knowledge and is not in touch with the living God, then an emphasis on the moral aspects of sin will not help him to get back to a true understanding of God, but may hinder such a true knowledge. And in the meantime it will not do him any good from a religious point of view that he is keeping the moral law merely for some lesser motive.

This does not mean that it is not a good thing to keep the moral law. But it does mean that keeping a moral law should not become mixed up with the Christian religion in its essential character. They are often inextricably muddled with the result that

---

[1] *A Shewing of God's Love*, ed. Anna Maria Reynolds, p. 50, sec. 17.
[2] P. 116.

many people are quite mistaken as to the nature of each. Each has its place so long as the limits of each are clearly appreciated.

It is here that the use of sacramental confession must also be seen in its true light. Its first and over-riding purpose is to bring to the penitent the assurance of the active forgiving love of God. Unless this is done the penitent may find in his confession wrong emphases which may hide rather than reveal the truth. It is for this reason that a highly schematic approach to his sinful acts can put the wrong ideas into his head and lead him to adopt a legalistic attitude when the whole operation ought to bring him to the opposite conviction. But if the main purpose is constantly kept in mind the practice of sacramental confession can be of the greatest benefit to many people.

One of the clearest conclusions of modern psychological research is that nobody really knows himself, that all of us are to some degree formed by stresses and experiences which are not present to the conscious mind. Where questions of sin and guilt are concerned, in particular, these unconscious elements can often be damaging to the integration of the personality. The inevitable consequence of these simple and universally accepted facts is that all need the advice of others in their spiritual life, and the confessional is the obvious place in which they can be recalled to the great truths of the Christian religion.

This does not mean that everything can be solved in the confessional—far from it. There are many people who have problems which can only be dealt with by a prolonged form of pastoral counselling or psychiatric help. They should not be encouraged to think that the confessional is the right place for such prolonged treatment. But in making their confessions they can receive guidance as to what help they do in fact need, and also accept the free forgiveness of God which is brought to them there, together with the particular grace which God provides through that sacrament.

"If forgiveness is the basis of the realization of fellowship with God, it means that forgiveness is both the essential foundation of the Christian life, and its continually active power."[1] This

[1] Aulén, op. cit., p. 292.

thoroughly Catholic statement by a modern Lutheran theologian brings us back to the place where we started our discussion of penitence. The true Christian tradition of sin and forgiveness has been overlaid by Latin legalism, Protestant scholasticism, and popular misrepresentation. Its recovery is an indispensable step for the growth of the spiritual life.

Prayer

13

Introductory

In discussing the subject of prayer, as in other parts of the spiritual life, it is necessary to be selective. The amount of literature on the subject through the centuries is immense, and no book which aims at being to some extent practical can do more than refer to small parts of it. As an academic exercise the literature may be divided up into different categories, according to national origin or historical period, or some other classification, but the result of such treatment is only too often to remove from the study the spirit of prayer and to turn it into a form of analysis.

It would also seem to be presumptuous for anyone to write about the subject of prayer who has not himself advanced far on the way which is described by the famous writers on the subject. But there is some risk that to adopt such an attitude is to confess that prayer is a matter for the specialist alone, and not for the ordinary Christian in his everyday life. It is, of course, true that no one can write fully about the "higher" states of prayer, as they are usually called, who has no experience of them. On the other hand it is important to realize that some experience of these states of prayer comes to many Christians at various stages of their life, and that they are not limited to those who have spent ten years in the desert, or who have subjected themselves to extreme mortifications.

The prayer life is normally divided in the Western tradition into three main stages, called respectively the purgative, the illuminative, and the unitive ways. We may readily acknowledge that this division does correspond to important facts in the prayer life, but it must then immediately be stated that they are not three stages which inevitably succeed one another, and that this categorization is, like many others, artificial. All three ways may be experienced to some degree or other at an early stage in the prayer life: illumination and union are the gifts of God. He does not withhold them from a soul until after the prescribed number of exercises. Every soul differs from every other soul, and there are some to whom God at once shows himself, or unites to himself, at the beginning of their spiritual journey.

The question of time in human terms does not necessarily apply in the way which we would expect. The progress in prayer of any particular person depends on the condition of his soul, its natural *attraits* and abilities, the condition of the will and the decision of God as to what treatment he should have. It is, therefore, dangerous for any Christian to think that for spiritual progress his prayer is necessarily bound to go through a fixed series of manoeuvres. The best analogy is that of growth. Prayer is growth in the love of God. In every person the capabilities of growth are different, the hindrances to growth vary, the speed of growth is not the same. In some plants the flowers come before the leaves, in others there is little stem, while in yet others there are no flowers at all except perhaps for one day before the plant dies. So it is with the human soul.

There is a permanent human tendency to try to enclose God in man's systems and to imply that if God does not follow what seems to us a logical order, this must be because his laws have been interfered with by some bad influence. Nothing could be further from the truth. God is greater than our logic, and greater than our little systems, into which we should like to fit him in a tidy manner. And it is often the good devoted Christians who make God appear small and small-minded by this attitude. The greatness, the lavishness, the generosity, and the supra-rational nature of God must always be present to the minds of those who wish to speak of his influence on the guidance of the prayer life.

On the other hand certain facts have been generally found to be true by those who have learnt much about prayer, and we must learn from them. There is always the danger of an unbalanced view, especially when a man is trying to analyse his own prayer life; that is one of the reasons why it is so important to have a director or adviser with whom he can discuss spiritual matters and have his own lack of balance put right. It is important to emphasize these points, but on the other hand it is also important not to jump to the opposite conclusion and to imagine that order has nothing to do with the life of prayer, and that all that is needed is a disordered good will. We are not surprised to find that there is rule and discipline to be observed in the life of prayer in a way parallel to what is required in physical or mental training.

To put the point in a sharp practical manner it may be expressed thus: meditation as a formal or semi-formal exercise is for most people a desirable and probably necessary part of their early prayer life. This must be recognized. But meditation must be left behind as soon as God shows some other way of prayer along which he wants to lead a soul. There is a temptation either to make meditation the be-all and end-all of the prayer life, a not uncommon mistake among certain Anglicans, or, on the other hand, to hold that meditation does not really matter much and the sooner it is dropped the better. Neither of these is correct, and a right balance must be sought between them.

14

The three Ways

Some writers on the spiritual life have discussed the ways of prayer as though they always followed the same pattern. This can be misleading, as we have seen. Yet it is well to know what this pattern is, and perhaps the Ignatian approach can put it in its clearest form. It is also important for readers to bear in mind that different writers use the same terms in different senses. Thus St Ignatius of Loyola uses the word "contemplation" to indicate a process which is the immediate result, and more or less part, of a meditation on the facts of the life of Christ. Others use it for an advanced type of prayer which is very simple in character. Some writers also distinguish between acquired and infused contemplation, reserving the latter term for the "highest" stages of mystical prayer.

For experts there is value in trying to distinguish between the various types of prayer and trying to relate them to one another. But attempts at systematization can lead even them astray. It is, for example, impossible to make an adequate distinction between acquired and infused contemplation without breaking up the spiritual life and in a sense alienating some of it from God. When an expert on St Ignatius writes: "Of extraordinary or infused contemplation S. Ignatius says little, for indeed it cannot be taught in books, but is a supernatural gift of God"[1] he makes a statement which is profoundly true. But it is just as true of the whole of the prayer life as it is of the extraordinary conditions to which he refers.

There is, moreover, a tendency in some quarters to regard what is extraordinary as in some way "higher" than the ordinary.

[1] W. H. Longridge, *The Spiritual Exercises of St Ignatius of Loyola.*

Why this should be it is difficult to say, since by the canons of judgement, which all the great saints adopt, the prayer life is to be judged, not by mystical states, trances, or extraordinary prayer experiences, but solely by the results which the prayer experience produces in the life of him who experiences it. The ordinary may in the eyes of God often be "higher" than the extraordinary, and in some ways this would seem to be in closer accord with the principle of the Incarnation, in which it is the fact that God became man, ordinary, fully human man, that makes it so important for each member of the human race.

The truth is that there are innumerable varieties of spiritual experience and methods of growth in prayer. Yet it is evident that systems which have been tried and found helpful by many earnest Christians have value for others who are also trying to tread the path of discipleship like them. Meditation will, therefore, be for most people a method to be used at the beginning of their prayer life, and quite probably during much of its later stages too. But the object of meditation, which may take many forms, is to enlighten the mind, to stimulate the imagination, and to draw forth from the person the desire to love God by applying the subject of the meditation to his own life. St Ignatius recommended ways of conducting meditation, which certainly will not suit all tastes or temperaments. Other writers have suggested other approaches. Each person must choose the method most suitable to himself.

There is a second purpose in meditation, namely the introduction into prayer of spiritual discipline especially that of thought. Order is needed in the spiritual life as in any other part of life, and effort has to be made to control the natural tendency to allow one's thoughts to run wild. Meditation provides a useful form of this discipline, without which growth in prayer is even more difficult than it need be.

All writers encourage those engaged in prayer not to tie themselves down to the meditation, but to be ready to leave it when God allows other movements to enter the soul. "Meditation" as a word merely means thinking carefully about some part of the Christian Faith, and is not to be regarded as an end in itself, though it must always form some part of a Christian's life, either in his prayer or outside it. Meditation is usually expected to move into affective prayer, described by Dom Vitalis Lehodey as "that which allows less space than meditation does *to considerations and more to the affections*".[1] Acts of love and other acts of affection become more frequent and easier.

Affective prayer in turn leads on to the prayer of simplicity in which very little is *done*, but in which the soul remains in loving attention to God, sometimes described as "active quiet" or in some similar phrase. It is not a merely passive attitude, even though there is very little action, and it is often important for ordinary people who naturally tend towards such prayer to understand that it is a very good form of prayer, and that it is not necessary in their prayer always to be doing something, so long as they are learning merely to love their Lord.

Then there are the various stages of mystical contemplation and particular experiences associated with it. Such states are not to be rigidly distinguished from other forms of prayer, and are often in some degree or other closely allied to them. Dom V. Lehodey, like others, makes a distinction between acquired and infused contemplation,[2] but it is not a satisfactory distinction, for it divides God's grace into ordinary and extraordinary, as though his grace was in some way a gift separate from his own nature. All prayer is the activity of God in the soul, adapted to the needs and capabilities of the particular person in question.

In his book on *The Spiritual Life*, Fr A. Tanquerey provides a complete systematization of its various aspects, but in doing so he does not succeed in overcoming the disadvantages to which we have already referred. Nevertheless we may learn from his treatment how the three ways are traditionally arranged. The purgative way, or the purification of the soul, includes mental prayer for beginners; the illuminative way, or progress in Christian virtues, includes affective prayer; while the unitive way covers infused contemplation following on the prayer of simplicity, and then other extraordinary mystical phenomena.

Those who wish earnestly to enter or progress in the life of

---

[1] *The Ways of Mental Prayer*, p. 179.   [2] Op. cit., p. 217.

prayer and who read any literature on the subject will certainly come across references to the above terms. They should not suppose that these matters are clearly and universally agreed in their bearings and practice. Moreover, it is highly undesirable that devout people should find themselves analysing their own spiritual life and trying to discover what stage on the road they have reached, for it is not a road of a predetermined length, nor is there *one* road for everyone. Some are led along by-paths which only God can find for the soul; some go by the highway which has been trodden by many before them; some go on foot, slowly plodding yet learning much which others miss; some go by car with the dangers which speed and careless driving can bring; while others are transported by air quickly to the destination to which God wants to bring them.

15

Growing in and through Prayer

Among the many descriptions of what prayer is, some are too static. They describe prayer as a state of contact with God, or conversation with him. So far as they go these ideas are good, but they can mislead if prayer is seen merely as a certain attitude on the part of the person praying, or a set of circumstances which has to be brought about.

Prayer is movement: that is a fact about the life of prayer which must never be overlooked or pushed into the background. This movement does not mean that prayer consists in doing things, in a kind of permanent activity in which the person concerned has constantly to be thinking of new acts to undertake, either spiritually or bodily. Prayer is movement in the sense that it is growth, in the sense that all life is movement. There is no standing still in any sort of life, whether physical, mental, or spiritual. Either the faculties of the person are growing and developing, or they are withering. Lack of movement is death.

The idea of spiritual growth then is at the root of prayer. But it is not a kind of self-culture in which we are constantly examining ourselves and trying to produce by conscious effort a one hundred per cent growth, like the advertisements which promise you a perfect body if you will only follow the course of physical exercise which such and such a he-man offers you. The result may be a revolting specimen of overdeveloped muscles, which may be admirable for photographs but are not much use for everyday life.

In prayer self-culture defeats its own purpose, because it breaks the basic rule of health in prayer—that he who loses his life shall find it. Self-culture in prayer, because it is self-centred, is self-defeating. Growth comes from devoting one's life through prayer to God, and leaving it to him to decide what rate and manner of growth is suitable for the person in question.

But in some ways prayer is like the body or mind. Exercise is indispensable if growth is to take place. It has to be regular and controlled, not left to the whims of the moment: it must be governed by rule and deliberate choice. It must face hardships and difficulties, so as to strengthen the muscles and will. It must be ready for suffering in the cause which matters more than all others, learning to do the will of God.

More will be said about this a little later. But the first thing to face in prayer is the need for discipline, for until this is accepted, it is not possible to make any progress in growth. It is like a child learning to use its legs. Until there is some discipline and control over the muscles there can be no progress in walking, still less in running. Advance corresponds to the measure in which discipline over the nerves and muscles is established.

So in prayer discipline over the activity of the soul, and over the time which it needs, is a prerequisite of growth. The nerves and muscles of the spiritual limbs must first be exercised and controlled, and then time must be given to their use. It would be thought strange if physical muscles were to be expected to grow strong without time being given to their use. So it is with spiritual powers. And since for many people spiritual activities tend to be pushed out altogether, this means that a time must be set aside for prayer each day, and constantly kept for this purpose.

When the plan for a time of spiritual exercise is left out for some reason, either through forgetfulness or because of more pressing business which could not be ignored, then it must be resumed at the earliest possible moment. It is strange how many people fall into the temptation of the devil to give up altogether a rule which they have lately made, because they have broken it once or twice. They say that it is no good and jettison the whole thing, thus doing themselves immense harm.

A rule is not something which has to be entirely kept or entirely abandoned. It is a guide to oneself of what one ought to do. It is made for the purpose of keeping an aim before one's eyes. It is, therefore, absurd to abandon it because of one or two failures to keep it: it ought rather to be held constantly before one's eyes as an aim which is reached as often as is possible. And the more it is dropped, the more it ought to be pursued. But it must be made with this caution: a rule, when made, ought not to be too difficult, but should be one which can normally be kept without too much difficulty. It should be a minimum rather than a maximum.

Part of the value of a system of meditation in prayer undoubtedly derives from the fact that it helps to discipline the prayer life, though, if persisted in too long, it may become a strait-jacket. At first in the prayer life some method of meditation is helpful, and it is most beneficial if it is not prolonged beyond the point where it is useful and creative. Order in prayer is also learnt through facing dryness and wandering thoughts and the way in which these are dealt with. The natural tendency of the human spirit is to give way to impatience when it fails at once to attain the objectives which it seeks. Discipline is a necessary ingredient in securing the steadiness which is a prime requirement for growth in spiritual things.

This conception of discipline is merely the application to the spiritual life of those principles which we find to be needed in all parts of human nature, whether body, mind, or spirit. The same natural laws of growth apply to all the parts, which are integrated with one another and cannot be regarded as watertight compartments with no connection between them. For the growth of mind and body exercise and discipline are needed; it is the same for the spirit. It is thus that purification is achieved— the overcoming of those elements in the life of man which stand in the way of complete dedication to the will of God.

16

There is need for
Indifference or Detachment

The use of the word "indifference" has come in modern times to mean a lack of interest, but this is not strictly its proper meaning. Indifference should mean impartiality, and when it is used in connection with the spiritual life it corresponds in meaning with another common word in spiritual writers, "detachment". Both words describe an attitude which is of great importance in the life of a Christian.

Because it is important to understand rightly this point, we must carefully guard against wrong interpretations. No one can or ought to be indifferent about the aim of his prayer life, which must be the growth of the spirit according to the will of God. That is the ruling object of everything for which the spiritual life is created. But within this overall aim the soul must be free from attachments which will have the effect of upsetting the soul and keeping it in a perpetual state of crisis and difficulty.

The virtues of indifference and detachment are basically those of right proportion in the spiritual life. There can be only one attachment in the life of the soul—attachment to God—in connection with which there must be detachment from everything else which is not God. This truth can be grasped by the intellect fairly easily. If there is indeed only one over-riding truth about life, that a man must cleave to God alone, then it is plainly true that all other things are to be valued only so far as they help towards the achievement of this aim. If they assist, they are to be used, and if they hinder they are to be rejected.

In practice a difficulty arises because at one stage in the spiritual life something may help, and at a later stage it may hinder, progress towards God. We find that in the early stages God gives his spiritual favours to those who are beginning their life of prayer, but later withholds them, because that is necessary at the stage they have reached. At the start it is good to encourage them on the way by such aids, but later on it is good to teach them to do without, so as to make their faith stronger and to train them to lean only upon God, rather than on his gifts.

Thus in the second stage the Christian learns to be indifferent to those pleasant experiences, when they are compared to the personal unity with himself that God wishes to give him. This is the virtue which is extolled by our Lord Jesus himself in the New Testament, when he emphasizes the need to give up things which are in themselves good in order to follow him in the higher good to which a man is called. "No man is worthy of me who cares more for father or mother than for me; no man is worthy of me who cares more for son or daughter; no man is worthy of me who does not take up his cross and walk in my footsteps. By gaining his life a man will lose it; by losing his life for my sake, he will gain it." (Matt. 10.37.)

From the words of Jesus we learn the need for indifference or detachment in two senses. First we are not to put our good and natural affections ahead of the duty of following Jesus Christ. It would, of course, be absurd to suppose that Jesus is telling us that we must abandon our duties to our families, and not bother about looking after our parents or our children. He is, as so often, pointing his lesson by the use of striking pictures, and the lesson is plain, namely that our affections for and our duties towards our families and other good and natural things can only rightly be ordered when they come second to that of doing the will of God, and of following Christ.

Jesus ends these words by framing the great law of the spiritual life, that he who loses his life for the sake of God will find it. Such is the law of love: it springs directly out of the law of love both in God and man. It is demonstrated conclusively in the life of Jesus himself, whose victory was won in the loss of his life on the cross. That is the way in which all victories of love are won—

by being lost, by self-giving to the uttermost, by drinking the cup which God has given to the bitter dregs.

There are many cases in which losing one's life in the service of Jesus has been shown in the care for an aged parent by a child, who has found in it the duty of self-sacrifice in the doing of God's will. Here it is not a case of caring for a parent more than for Jesus, but caring for Jesus and for the parent in him. The life of the child is lost in the care for the parent, but is found in the new life which comes only from doing the will of God.

The right way of looking at things requires indifference or detachment because it is God's will that must be done, and in doing it the natural desires and affections which we have must be regarded as secondary. The virtue of detachment is in short the capacity to see things in their right proportions, in the light of God's love and of the example and teaching of Jesus.

While a true view does not mean abandoning our family duties, it does mean keeping our natural family affections in balance, simply because of the principles which we have mentioned. It is possible for every good human thing to be turned into something bad, by making it into an idol, by putting it into the place of God. So the love of a parent for his children can be bad if everything else is thought to be unimportant compared with what he thinks to be the good of his own offspring. In such a case he is not only harming himself, but also harming his children, by inculcating into them by his own attitude the idea that their wishes or needs are to be preferred above anything else.

We do not excuse bad actions by saying that they were done for someone else's benefit, whether that someone else is a close relative or a stranger. All the good intentions and affections come from God, but like all else they are given so that they may be used for his purpose, for unless they are so used, they bring nothing but unhappiness and frustration.

Indifference and detachment, then, in everyday life mean that we must not put anything in the place of God, but see all things and all people in relation to him, and be ready to give up what we want if it is shown to be God's will.

In the spiritual life the same principle applies. We must never allow ourselves to become attached to anything except God and his will. If we allow ourselves to value most of all the things we enjoy about prayer, or the things which we get out of it, or even the sense of self-sacrifice as an achievement, then we are in fact putting something else in the place which God and his will should alone occupy.

St Francis de Sales says on this point:

> So our hearts in the beginning of their devotion love God that they may be united and become agreeable unto him, and imitate him in that he hath loved us for all eternity; but by little and little being formed and exercised in holy love, they are imperceptibly changed. In lieu of loving God in order to please God, they begin to love him for the pleasure they take in the exercises of holy love; and instead of falling in love with God, they fall in love with the love they bear him, and stand affected to their own affections. They no longer take pleasure in God, but in the pleasure they find in his love.[1]

He goes on to stress the importance of submission to the will of God—of resignation to it whatever it may bring, whether pleasant or disagreeable experiences, being sure that God knows what is best for the soul and that he will guide it in its development.

Indifference, detachment, or resignation, in the sense which we have been describing it, is also an important attitude so as to avoid too much introspection in our prayer. Many people are always asking themselves questions about the state of their spiritual life, as to whether this or that is good or bad, or how they can know that their motives are pure, or how they can know that something in their prayer is to be thought an advance. But these questions do harm because it is not possible for any person to answer them reliably, though they can find help from discussion with some spiritual guide. It is through the cultivation of an attitude of trust in God and indifference to other things, that we gradually learn to rely solely upon him, and to accept whatever he sends or permits in the growth of our spiritual personality.

[1] *On the Love of God*, bk 9, ch. 9.

17

The Pleasures of Prayer

The attainment of indifference, of which we have just spoken, comes with practice, and the practice involves some experiences which are easy and pleasant and others which are difficult and hard. But without them it would be impossible to achieve that detachment which is necessary for growth in the life of love with God. For it is not a theoretical notion but an intensely practical virtue.

To some people prayer brings satisfaction and delight, to others it is a hard struggle throughout their earthly life. Most Christians have a mixture of both, just as ordinary earthly life is made up of experiences of joy and sadness at the extremes, and dullness in the centre. In prayer it is not unusual to experience satisfaction at the beginning, and then later to find it all the harder when the pleasure of praying disappears.

On the spiritual plane it is like the act of falling in love on the natural level. The intense pleasure which is experienced in falling in love is apparently given to man by God for the purpose of starting two people off in the right way on what is a lifelong pilgrimage together. The initial impetus is so powerful because there is need for mobilization of all the resources to launch the marriage rightly and to keep it going at the start. But every thinking person knows that the problems of marriage are in many cases tedious, and usually prolonged. The love which is to be built up in married life is something far deeper and less turbulent than the feelings of those young people who have fallen in love with each other. If their marriage is to be successful they have to see the joys and pleasures of it in their right proportions, as means of helping them to a deeper understanding and love of one another which is essentially independent of those sensations. It is only in the measure that they become detached from those pleasures, in other words that they cease to lean on them or to regard them as the most important element in their married life, that they will be successful in creating a truly Christian marriage, based on self-giving love.

There is no need for an apology in applying this analogy to the spiritual life. The love of a man and a woman for each other in its highest forms has often been used as a picture of the love of and for God, as in the Song of Songs. Moreover, it is only to be expected that the laws, which we see are made by God for men on the natural plane, should be reproduced on the spiritual plane. (This contrast between natural and spiritual is not satisfactory, since it is difficult to escape the implication that the spiritual is unnatural. On the contrary the spiritual is equally natural in the sense that it is part of our human nature, and grows within the framework of what God has provided for the whole man.)

In the spiritual life, then, pleasure in prayer is often (though not always) experienced in the earlier life of prayer for a parallel purpose to that of falling in love, namely in order to give sufficient impetus to the will to begin solidly and regularly, and thus to establish a habit and rule which will not be overthrown at the first obstacles which are met. But the important part of the spiritual life lies elsewhere, not in the emotions or pleasant sentiments, but in the degree to which the will is hardened and firmly set on following the will of God, and on submitting to his ordinances.

If we read of the experiences of the saints who have been far advanced in the spiritual life and the practice of prayer we find that their teaching about visions and delights is the same. Pleasures must not be regarded as of importance, they must not be valued for themselves or clung to, but the Christian must be detached from them, and use them for strengthening the basic attachment of the will to God. The saints point out that the devil can appear in the guise of an angel of light and that it is impossible to say at any particular moment that this vision is from God and that from the devil. It is the attitude of detachment which can bring good out of such visions from whatever source they come. For if they come from the Devil it means that they have no effect in causing pride or self-satisfaction, but that they are turned into instruments of good against the Devil's wish by inducing an increase in humility. If they come from God they come in order to teach the same lesson of detachment by resisting the temptation to value them for themselves.

Fr W. H. Longridge, s.s.j.e., in commenting on *The Spiritual Exercises of St Ignatius of Loyola* makes this point when considering the meditation on the two standards, the standard of Christ and the standard of the Devil. Speaking of the snares and deceits of the devil, he says that the Devil sometimes even simulates the voice of Christ himself "and allures us to things which appear good, or at least not evil, but which will in reality, if we listen to him, lead us unawares and little by little away from Christ and into sin".[1] His remarks have a much wider application than that which we have been considering, but they rest on the same principle.

The underlying truth is that growth in prayer depends ultimately on not wanting the enjoyment of what we are undertaking. Detachment has to go to the uttermost limits. We have to long for God and God alone without the pleasures which we think this may bring. We have to give up the desire for the pleasures of prayer, and even the desire for the pleasure of giving up the pleasures. A modern writer, Thomas Merton, has well expressed the point:

> The secret of interior peace is detachment. Recollection is impossible for the man who is dominated by all the confused and changing desires of his own will. And even if those desires reach out for the good things of the interior life, for recollection, for peace, for the pleasures of prayer, if they are no more than natural and selfish desires they will make recollection difficult and even impossible.
>
> You will never be able to have perfect interior peace and recollection unless you are detached even from the desire of peace and recollection. You will never be able to pray perfectly until you are detached from the pleasures of prayer.
>
> If you give up these desires and seek one thing only, God's will, He will give you recollection and peace in the middle of labour and conflict and trial.[2]

[1] Op. cit., p. 238.   [2] *Seeds of Contemplation*, p. 75.

18

Suffering and Hardship
in Prayer

The need to become detached from pleasure and agreeable experience in prayer cannot in fact be met merely by thinking about it. It can only come by practice, by having to meet the temptations which tend to the opposite result and by overcoming them. One can do something to prepare the mind and will to meet the temptation when it comes, and to take the right attitude towards it. But the training of the spirit, like the training of the body, has to be undergone in actual reality if the spirit is to become really fit and strong.

The bodily parallel is a good method of explanation. St Paul uses the same figure in his well-known passage to the Corinthians (1 Cor. 9.24): "You know (do you not?) that at the sports all the runners run the race, though only one wins the prize. Like them, run to win! But every athlete goes into strict training. They do it to win a fading wreath; we, a wreath that never fades. For my part, I run with a clear goal before me; I am like a boxer who does not beat the air; I bruise my own body and make it know its master, for fear that after preaching to others I should find myself rejected."

A man would be thought to be mad who said that he was doing nothing to his body in order to prepare for a stiff race, but that he spent a long time thinking himself into the right frame of mind and that this was the whole of his training. Even with the knowledge which we have to-day of the power of mind over body, we should hardly expect him to win a race in normal circumstances against those who had gone into training seriously. In order to make our body fit for whatever it is called upon to do, it must itself have the necessary training; otherwise it will fail at the critical moment.

The muscles of the body have to be developed and its resources put into working order for the task it has to meet. It has to grow to the stage at which it can discharge that task, and it can do so only by being trained. Such training can be done in one of two ways: either it can be a carefully planned and regulated training under the supervision of an expert; or in other circumstances the training can come through the everyday work which has to be done, through which the body is developed, as when a man who is engaged in physical work every day finds his body more and more adapted for the purpose of doing it well.

The same principles apply to the spiritual life. It is a chimera to imagine that the detachment and determination which are necessary in the life of prayer can be achieved merely by thinking that it would be nice to have them, any more than physical capabilities can. Such a spiritual condition can be achieved only by training, by actually meeting the conditions and overcoming the difficulties which they involve. One should not conclude from this that advance in the spiritual life is a kind of self-culture which merely depends on doing regular routine exercises—far from it. The analogy which we have used must not be pressed too far. There is one point only which is to be noted here, namely that our learning of detachment—through the grace of God and the help of the Holy Spirit—in our prayer life can only come in normal circumstances through having to face the actual conditions in which it has to be exercised.

So in the first place, as we saw in the last section, it has to meet pleasant experiences and learn that they are to be used for the lesson of detachment, and not to be sought for their own sake. We could not learn such a lesson if we never had such an experience.

And in the second place it is necessary for the spirit to meet and grapple with suffering and hardship in order again to learn to resist and overcome the temptation to give up whenever such hardships occur. The two methods by which this is done are closely parallel to those we have seen in connection with physical training: first, the regular adoption of a training schedule under the guidance of someone who is qualified to give such guidance— a spiritual director of experience and wisdom; and second, the acceptance of the buffets and problems of everyday life as a means for spiritual advance, learning more and more to want only the will of God.

There is no difference of opinion whatever among the great spiritual writers as to the absolute necessity of undergoing spiritual hardships in the way of following Christ. All testify to their inevitability and to their great usefulness. And we do not here speak of external mortifications of the flesh, or self-infliction of hardships, but of the difficulties and obstacles which are an inescapable part of growth in the spiritual life of prayer. Fr Longridge may again be quoted for putting the point well:

> We are not to think that our meditation has been badly made because we have had few or no lights or consolations, or because we have been much tried with wandering thoughts, aridity, or even diabolical temptations. If, in spite of these obstacles we have really tried our best to persevere the full time in prayer, and to reject wandering thoughts and temptations, however violent and insistent, to be patient in dryness, and to keep ourselves as best we can in the presence of God, then we may be sure our meditation has not been unfruitful.[1]

In these words he is speaking of an early stage in the life of prayer and is dealing with simple things, but the principle which he is explaining applies throughout the spiritual life from the first moment when we kneel down to try to give our wills to God, to the point when a saint is raised to the highest of spiritual states by the grace of God. The most common suffering in prayer is just that which Fr Longridge describes: wandering thoughts, dryness, and even evil thoughts. There is more suffering through these than there is through more sensational spiritual trials.

Many people find it difficult to believe that wandering thoughts and dryness can possibly be part of growth in prayer, or have any part in the plan of God for the spiritual life. But this is because

[1] Op. cit., p. 72.

they see prayer primarily as something which gives them satisfaction, or as what they often call "helpful", which usually means the same thing, rather than as one stage in a long process of ridding the spirit of self-centredness so that it may cling to God and his will alone. There are some Christians who have persisted in prayer throughout their whole life without any of those experiences which have meant much to others in their early stages. Their prayer seemed cold and lifeless, and they have never had a feeling of satisfaction about it. Yet they have persisted, and those who observe them from outside have seen and continue to see how God greatly blesses them in developing their Christian character, and blesses those who know them. Yet all the time they themselves have been ignorant of any such knowledge.

Suffering and hardship is, as innumerable saints testify, the safest way of prayer. Consolations in prayer are dangerous, as we have seen earlier, but sufferings are safe in that we cannot possibly misunderstand their functions. We know for certain that whether they come from God, or from the world, or the devil, they are God-given opportunities for helping us forward in our pilgrim's progress. Jean Pierre Camus in *The Spirit of St Francis de Sales* wrote:

A Sister complained to the Bishop of her inward desolation and dryness in prayer. Instead of consoling her, he replied: "For my part I always think dried fruits better than those which are moist; it was in a barren and dry land that God called forth the water-springs, and that He showed forth His Power and Glory. Manna, that heavenly food, that bread of angels, was a mere dry little seed; but when the Israelites insisted on changing it for flesh, while the meat was yet in their mouths the heavy wrath of God came upon them."

Few people accept what is, nevertheless, a great truth, that a faithful, upright soul is more closely and intimately united to God amid desolation and loneliness, than in sensible devotion and consolation.[1]

This teaching springs directly out of the New Testament and echoes the words of Jesus, so often repeated, that his way is that of bearing a cross and finding triumph through suffering. His words

[1] Op. cit., p. 19.

were perfectly shown in his deeds. His suffering in prayer is graphically described in the Garden of Gethsemane and on the cross itself. Are we to think that we can follow in his footsteps and in our prayer avoid the dust and toil of the way of the cross? The question answers itself.

19

Calm is a need in Spiritual Things

Introspection is a snare in the spiritual life because it is apt to result in anxiety. It is a continual temptation to anyone who cares about spiritual things to be always wanting to examine himself in order to gauge the point which has been reached, to analyse the experiences which he has undergone and to be able to judge whether he is progressing or regressing. It is a natural desire to wish to know how one is getting on, whether in spiritual or in any other things. But in the spiritual life it is something which must be avoided as much as possible.

For this reason it is often not particularly helpful to have read many books about the life of prayer. It is possible to know the contents of all the books without having advanced one step along the road. No one can adequately judge of his own spiritual condition, and for this reason it is important for all to have a spiritual director or guide who can and will provide advice, and who will be able to judge spiritual conditions from an independent viewpoint.

Anxiety about one's spiritual condition is always a sign of being over-preoccupied with oneself. One of its dangers lies in the fact that it often appears under the guise of humility or self-deprecation. An over-emphasis on penitence can lead to such anxiety, which is in a way a lack of faith in the love of God and the forgiveness brought through Jesus Christ. It becomes easily an inverted kind of pride, which says in effect that *my* sins are too great for such forgiveness, or that *I* am too unworthy to be able to partake fully in the divine love. Thus the ego is put in the centre of the picture where Christ alone ought to be found.

That is one kind of anxiety. Another springs from impatience in the life of prayer. We feel that we are not getting along fast enough and that this is a serious fault. We then begin to worry about whether our technique is quite right, or whether we ought to do this or that. But this worry too is a form of self-centredness since it shows in effect that we are not satisfied to leave our progress in the hands of God unless it measures up to the standards which we have set for ourselves in such matters.

From our earliest years we have been told when running races not to look over our shoulders to see how our position compares with the next person in the race, but to keep our eye on the tape and run our best. So in the life of prayer we are not to compare ourselves to other people, whether they are imaginary people from books, or real people whom we know or have heard about. God has his own plan for each, and each person differs in his make-up from everyone else, and must, therefore, be led along the path which is alone suitable for him.

What we can learn from others are the basic principles of the spiritual life, such as that anxiety is wrong, and that calm and confidence in God are all important, so long as we are following the advice of some spiritual person. Forcing one's prayer life is also wrong, since it introduces strain which is akin to anxiety into its centre. Père Charles de Condren puts the matter thus: "Do nothing by forcing your intellect or your spirit, but with true faith that you can, with Jesus Christ, by the virtue of His Spirit, do all that is useful to God's glory and the good of your soul"; or again: "Flee all disquietude of spirit, and all constraint in spiritual things. . . . Oh, how great a secret is it in the spiritual life to belong to God without attachment to anything else and *without choice of any means by which to honour Him*, but with a perfect will to use for His Glory whatsoever His Providence may cause us to meet with, and to be one with Him in His Will thus."[1]

"We must do all by love and nothing by force: it is better to love obedience than to fear disobedience"—that is how St Francis de Sales puts it[2] and points us to the reason why force, anxiety, and lack of calm are wrong, namely because they

[1] Quoted by Henri Bremond, *A Literary History of Religious Thought in France*, vol. iii, p. 339. [2] *Œuvres*, xii, 363.

betoken a lack of love in full trust in him who is loved. It shows a certain failure of that loving trust which it is the whole object of prayer to increase and unfold in the form of loving submission to the will of God whatever it may be.

It is easier to state what is desirable than to put it into effect, especially in the case of persons naturally prone to distrust themselves, and over-ready to think themselves wrong. The best advice in these cases is that those who find themselves subject to this particular temptation should direct their thoughts to God alone, making acts of loving submission in the form of short prayers, in which God is the centre rather than themselves. Moreover, some can be helped by returning, when in this state, to meditating on some aspects of the life of our Lord and thus fill the mind with thoughts of him rather than with those of self.

But it must also be recognized that the cure does not take place in a moment and that it may need long and determined persistence before God helps us out of the trough. Patience is part of our need: it is an essential element in the spiritual calm needed for growth in prayer. Impatience is the very reverse of the spirit of prayer for it shows a wish to dictate to God as to how he ought to deal with the soul, whereas it is the acceptance of his will which is the secret of all true prayer.

It is hardly necessary to say that in cases of unrest and anxiety the regular receiving of the sacrament of the Lord's Body and Blood, and of his forgiveness through the sacrament of Penance, are both important parts of overcoming our inner restlessness. Through them we receive the outward signs and seals of his forgiving and nourishing grace, the proof that God himself is in charge of our spiritual lives and gives us what we need to grow up into him.

But there are yet other kinds of anxiety, which spring unbidden and more or less uncontrollable from the depths of our emotional nature. No choice is made by the person concerned as to whether to be anxious or not, but he is assailed by all kinds of fears and unrest, perhaps out of the depth of his unconscious mind. Such fears may and often do spring from repressions which have their root in childhood, and it has to be plainly recognized and accepted that they cannot be banished merely by an act of the will. There is no easy technique by which they can be removed in a moment. If such anxiety states are deep-rooted and extreme, it may be necessary or desirable for a person to have psychiatric treatment in the form of psychoanalysis, which will expose the origin of the repression and thus exorcize its spirit by revealing its nature. But most people cannot in practice resort to this sort of treatment, either for lack of time or of money, and for the most part we are not in such a serious state that such prolonged treatment is necessary.

What then can be done? A first step of immense importance has been taken when the mind recognizes the truth that these anxiety states are in fact irrational and that they deny in our emotions the truths about God and his nature which we know to be true. This recognition does not immediately get rid of the emotion. We may have to live with these emotions for long periods, but they can be largely deprived of their power over us by acceptance. This is a key word throughout the spiritual and emotional life. It does not mean accepting them as good or even as neutral: it means not trying to pretend that they are not there, looking them full in the eye and examining them impartially, so far as we can do so. We say to ourselves that, however much we would like it to be otherwise, these emotions and restrictions are in fact part of the raw material with which we must deal in building our spiritual life. We know that God understands the whole thing: he sees into our backgrounds and notes the origins of these things without having to resort to a psychoanalyst to find out. He, therefore, equally knows that we cannot help having them, and consequently attaches no blame or guilt to these emotions, even when they are emotions of blaming ourselves or feeling guilty. If we may put it so, God sees us and loves us and wants to know what we are going to do with the emotions and other reactions which we have.

If we pretend we do not have them, we are running away from the truth about ourselves, and that will not get us anywhere useful spiritually. We cannot hide them from God who sees the secrets of our hearts, and it is unhealthy to try to hide them from ourselves. This is the first thing which has to sink deeply into our souls, and we may profitably use many hours of prayer over long periods of time letting this truth sink into our minds and hearts— that God knows the secrets of our hearts, and with them all in his mind is loving us into closer companionship with himself.

This will do much to enable calm in the right sense to begin to come to our soul. And, although it sounds paradoxical to say so, it is possible to have the true calm of the spiritual life at the same time as the emotional disturbances which we have been describing. For the spiritual calm of which we are speaking is nothing else but a choice of the will to rely on God and to trust him. This can be done even when the disturbances are present. It is not so much the presence of these worries which abolishes the calm, but the wrong choice of the will when it decides to entertain the worries and to give attention to them instead of to God.

Many of these worries stem from some kind of fear, very often, as we have seen, hidden fears which we ourselves are not in a position to analyse. Self-analysis is not something which we should encourage, although it is an ever present temptation to almost all of us. Its bad result, as is clear to anyone who thinks about it, is that self-analysis has the effect of setting ourselves in the centre of the picture at the very moment when we are supposed to be devoting ourselves to the task of setting God in the centre. We do often receive illumination about ourselves in our prayer, but it is always a derivative illumination. In other words light is thrown on ourselves from our contemplation of God and his work. It is only when we are not trying to throw light on ourselves, but only to seek God's will, that the truth about ourselves becomes manifest, almost as it seems by accident.

So, strange as it may seem, we may be inwardly calm in the midst of stormy emotions or anxieties which assail us independently of our wills. It is our choice that matters, not our unwilled worries. And if we gently and persistently realize this in the presence of God week after week, and year after year, he will help us to build something strong and creative out of the very unsatisfactory material which we present to him when we come to kneel at his feet.

20

In Prayer the Consecration of the Will is all-important

It will be clear from earlier discussion of the general subject that in prayer the will is the centre of the activity of the person. Fr W. H. Longridge in commenting on the spiritual exercises of St Ignatius in special connection with difficulties which we encounter in prayer makes the matter clear:

> It teaches the true method of overcoming the repugnance we feel to embracing the will of God when it is opposed to our natural desires. That method is to pray earnestly, and again and again, even though our lower nature shrinks and fears lest the prayer should be granted, that God would give us grace to make the sacrifice, and to protest before Him that we are ready to do so if it should be His will. This kind of prayer is most pleasing to God, and is of sovereign efficacy for overcoming ourselves. It was thus that our Lord prayed in the garden, "Not as I will, but as Thou wilt.". . . Even if it should seem to us that in forcing ourselves to make such prayers we are using words only, without any real desire of the heart accompanying them, still we must not think that such words are fruitless. Far from it. For God looks to our efforts far more than to our successes. Success is His gift to us, the struggle is our gift to Him. *It is our wills that He wants, not our feelings.* [Our italics.] And these words which seem to us so dry, and cost us so much effort, are true acts of the will, and are of more value to God, and often of more profit to our souls, than many warm feelings and consolations.[1]

Statements of this kind are alien to many Christians who have somehow got it into their heads that, if they do not have warm feelings, their prayer is no good. They have to mean what they say, is the way in which it is commonly put. But it is impossible

[1] *The Spiritual Exercises of St Ignatius of Loyola*, p. 114.

to discover any rational cause why this should be so. Why should a prayer be a better prayer because "we mean what we say"? If we analyse this phrase, we find that its true meaning is that we only think prayers are worth while when we have a feeling inside ourselves that we are doing it the right way: in other words that the test of prayer is to be the feeling which we have within our own selves, and therefore the test of prayer becomes our own satisfaction, instead of it being the measure of our conformity to God.

It is strange that these standards should be applied to prayer when they would never be applied to any other occupation. In the physical world we do not say that our cutting down of a tree is only truly done when we feel like it, when "we mean what we are doing" and like it. The test of whether we are cutting the tree down is in the strokes which we make with the axe at the command of our will. It is the same in the mental sphere. The test of whether we are doing a mathematical problem is not whether we feel we are doing it *con amore*, but whether we are in fact working out the calculations so as to reach the answer, and this depends exclusively on our will, on our choice, decision, or determination. So in the spiritual life the acts of prayer are valid and useful in so far as they express our will, not according to whether we are enjoying them or not, or whether we are feeling that "we mean what we say". The fact that we are saying it as an act of the will proves that we mean what we say at the deepest level of all, just as the fact that we are doing a mathematical problem proves that we want to do it with our will, even when the rest of our nature is rebelling against it.

There is no difference of opinion of any kind among the great teachers of the Christian life on this point. The remarks made by Fr Longridge not only present the teaching of St Ignatius, but they reproduce in essence a permanent part of spiritual teaching right through the Christian centuries. At different epochs the truth has been expressed in different ways. For example the teachers of prayer in the Protestant bodies in the sixteenth to eighteenth centuries for the most part put their teaching in a much more emotional way than is common in the Catholic tradition, though emotion is also to be found there in another guise. But when the teaching is analysed it is found to boil down to the same thing wherever the will is concerned, namely that dedication of the will is in the final analysis the decisive thing.

A good example of this is found in Philip Doddridge (1702–51) a Nonconformist divine and hymn writer. Here are some words from chapter 21 of *The Rise and Progress of Religion in the Soul*:

> Too great a stress is commonly laid on the flow of affections; and, for want of this, a Christian, who is ripened in grace, and greatly advanced in his preparation for glory, may sometimes be ready to lament imaginary rather than real decays, and to say, without any just foundation: "Oh that it were with me as in months past!" Therefore you can hardly be too frequently told, that religion consists chiefly, "*in the resolution of the will for God, and in a constant care to avoid whatever we are persuaded he would disapprove, to dispatch the work he has assigned to us in life, and to promote his glory in the happiness of mankind*". [Original italics].

Others say the same thing, though sometimes it is put in a way not quite so clear as this, and when we find, as we so often do, that the Christian men of prayer agree in the fundamental requirements of the spiritual life, we cannot doubt the authority of their teaching.

But this stress on the importance of the will does not mean that we raise ourselves to God by a spiritual effort of our own—any such idea would be a serious mistake and tend to injure the inner reality of prayer. For our prayer is an exercise in *submitting* our wills rather than in *raising* them up, it is an act of recognizing that God alone can teach us and give us growth in his love and that this can only come by the disappearance from our lives of a will aimed at our own selfish desires. This act of will is not a species of pulling ourselves up by hauling on our own spiritual shoe strings: it is a constant series of acts of submission to God as an expression of that love for him which we wish to show in our love.

Nor does it mean that God does not give us a deep satisfaction or conviction, which might in some circumstances be given the name of "feeling". Those who tread the path of God do enter into the heritage of "that peace of God which passeth all understanding", but this is something that we cannot acquire by our own efforts: it is the free gift of God, and is, so to speak, a by-product of something else, namely the attempt to consecrate our wills to God. The point about our feelings in prayer is that we must never go to prayer for the sake of trying to win nice feelings, and we must never judge our prayer by whether we have nice feelings or not. If God sees that we need a sense of deep satisfaction of contact with him he will give it to us, but the character of our prayer does not depend on any such gift. He may equally withhold it. That is why we must be indifferent in the spiritual sense to satisfaction in ourselves from prayer, knowing that prayer is absolutely indispensable for growth in the life of God's love, which is first and last shown in the identification of our will with his.

Yet the strain of the will which can undo the calm of the soul is not part of the submission of which we speak. Straining the will, making efforts of will, are a disguised return to relying on the feelings rather than on will: we say to ourselves that unless we are straining our will we are not really doing anything with it, and that the only way we know that this is so is by feeling the strain. This is another subtle temptation to be avoided, and we may note that temptations are often much better side-stepped than overcome by a wrestling clinch. Our will is shown by what we do, not by the immensity of its own effort, but purely and simply by its readiness calmly and quietly to submit to God and to await his gifts of trial or peace.

21

Resolution and Persistence

In any important task of life all will admit that resolution and persistence are indispensable in achieving one's aim: yet in prayer it is often undervalued, and sometimes even decried. As in many other aspects of the spiritual life, parallels from everyday life can be illuminating teachers.

If it is vitally important for us to reach a certain point by a certain time, we know that we can only do it by walking steadily and at a minimum pace from now until the time we arrive. If the call is of sufficient urgency, if for example our presence might be necessary to save the life of a child, we shall set out with determination and, whatever may be the obstacles, we shall continue until we get to our destination. The only thing which would stop us would be physical force greater than we could overcome. There might be many difficulties: the nature of the ground might be hard or rough, causing pain; the weather might be bad with snow or rain; or we might have difficulties from within ourselves, physical shortcomings from unaccustomed exercise and suffering from that cause; or mental anxieties and worries as to whether we should arrive on time. But if the need were great enough our determination would match it.

In prayer the need is of a greater urgency than any merely earthly crisis can produce. The need is for our own eternal health and salvation; but not only that, it is for the help and guidance of others too, for we must not see our spiritual life as a form of self-culture which is only for our own benefit. Through us God intends to bring his saving love to others, and for this prayer is indispensable, being the *sine qua non* of spiritual growth.

In our earthly example there is a difference from the spiritual activity of prayer, because a physical act would normally depend almost entirely on our own efforts, though we could of course receive great strengthening from the sense of the presence and help of God. But in prayer it depends even more on God's action, for in coming to him in prayer we put ourselves in his hands entirely. But he cannot do anything with us and for us unless our will has been given to him, that is, unless we have definitely chosen to try to give ourselves to him, and by doing so asked for his help and submitted to his will. God will not force himself on us.

The act of free will is the unlocking of the love of God for us. He stands at the door and knocks, ready to come in and sup with anyone who will open to him. But the door must be opened by the person whose door it is: God will not batter the door and insist on coming in, if the will of the person concerned has not made the free choice to invite him to come in. So the act of will must be made, and it must be continued.

The act of choice or of free will in asking God to come into our lives and to rule them is not one thing, which is done at a certain time on a certain day and then discontinued. It is done at a certain time on a certain day, but it then has to be continually renewed: it must become a constantly repeated act so that it becomes continuous in our lives even when we are not consciously thinking of it. It is only in this way that our will remains directed towards God, it is only thus that our invitation for him to come into our lives is a standing invitation, and not merely one which is intermittent. For God cannot come in and dwell in our hearts unless the invitation is a standing invitation.

How is this shown in practice? It is shown by resolution and persistence in prayer. Prayer being the vital activity in which we come to love God and receive his love ourselves, it is the sign by which we show what our choice really is. In prayer it is not so much the case that persistence will get us somewhere by our own efforts, but that our determination to persist in our time of prayer is the sign that our will has chosen God, and is absolutely determined not to make any other choice, and not to give him up.

It is, therefore, of great importance that whatever may seem to be the result or lack of result of our prayer we should persist in giving our time of prayer to God. We should not give up even when we are totally dry spiritually, or when we seem to have nothing but wandering thoughts. For God, as we know, looks on the heart, he sees our will, he knows whether or not we are trying to cling to him, and in many cases our trials become a test as to whether or not we really want to submit to God's will, or whether we are merely trying to seek some selfish spiritual satisfaction in our prayer.

Sometimes the obstacles which we meet in prayer—perhaps almost always—are the results of our own sinful past, or short-comings which are the product of our own failures or omissions. In this case the importance of not giving way to them is obvious, for it is only by persisting that there is the least chance of over-coming the difficulties, which we ourselves have created. And although some of them may be the product of acts, which in the past have been against the will of God, yet in these as in other evil situations God can make good out of them. He can and does bring good out of evil, and every event is an opportunity to learn more of him and to come closer to him and hence to what he wants us to be.

We must realize that there are some who have had to persist in prayer through decades without being granted any emotional assistance: their prayer has seemed to be dull and without fire, but they have persisted. What has been the result of this? Quite simply their lives have been transformed, and there are perhaps more examples of sanctity being granted by God to those who have persisted in the desert than to those who have found their way to be placed in pleasant groves and flowering glades.

Our will is not right unless it is expressed in resolution and persistence, for without them our act of will is merely word and not deed. We are not ourselves capable of judging whether or not our prayer is beneficial to us, least of all of deciding that because it does not give us the experience we want, it is useless. If persistence in prayer is part of our lives, God can and will use it to make us in the image of his Son.

22

Past, Present, and Future

In the spiritual life a proper attitude to past, present, and future is important, and may affect considerably the health of our souls. It is not easy for everyone to achieve, and whether it is hard or not to get a proper balance depends on the temperament of the individual person, or—what amounts to much the same thing—the particular stresses and strains to which he is subject from his own unconscious personality.

The New Testament has guide posts in these matters, and can show us the way to a right balance. As for the past we learn throughout the whole Bible that there are two attitudes which stand out as necessary in the right relations of a man with God. The first is an attitude of thankfulness which springs from the recognition of the good things which God has done for him in the past. These good things are not confined to his private benefits, but are to be extended to the whole of God's saving activity in history.

So we find at the heart of the right religion of the Jews the constant remembrance of the wonderful works which God has done for them, both in creation and in delivering his own people and looking after them during their long history. Perhaps this outlook could hardly be better put than in the words of the General Thanksgiving in the Anglican Prayer Book where we give thanks to God "for all thy goodness and loving-kindness to us and to all men. We bless thee for our creation, preservation, and all the blessings of this life: but above all for thine inestimable love in the redemption of the world by our Lord Jesus Christ, for the means of grace, and for the hope of glory."

The other part of a Christian's attitude to the past is part of this

147

general thanksgiving, but is concerned more with his own particular reasons for gratitude to God. In the first place he will remember the many mercies which he has received from God, applying to himself the same kind of considerations which we have been noting in the world at large. But in particular he thinks of the free forgiveness which God has extended to him, forgiving him all his sins, of which he has repented, and thus arming him with the redeeming love of God.

But in thus viewing the past, the Christian man does so in order to increase his love of God in the present and so to serve him the better. He does not dwell on the past or "live in the past" as the expression goes. Too much attention to the past can be harmful, and it is always bad when it consists in dwelling on one's sins and giving too much attention to them. Often such attention is excused by saying that it is done to increase repentance, but in most cases this means that its purpose is to increase emotional reaction from sin, which can often cover a hidden desire to dwell on the sin rather than on the forgiveness.

Like St Paul (Phil. 3.13) we should "forget what is behind me and reach out for that which lies ahead". It is a mistake to spend too much time in self-examination of ourselves which involves recalling to our minds and imaginations past sins, for once we know the forgiveness of God, we only recall our past sinfulness in order to rejoice in his loving pardon. The teaching of Jesus himself, without spelling out the warning in so many words, is clearly concerned to inculcate this same attitude, which permits us to escape from the bondage of our past sins into the glorious liberty of the children of God.

The great writers of the spiritual life teach the same lesson, and we find many of them warning those to whom they write of the undesirability, especially in beginners, of a tendency to spend too much time repenting of past sins. It is one of the benefits of the sacramental system of the Church that through confession before a priest we can make a definite spiritual gesture of leaving our sins behind us, when we receive the assurance of God's forgiveness.

But if we are not to spend too much time thinking of the

past, neither are we to spend too much time gazing into the future. Our Lord has clear instructions for us here, "So do not be anxious about tomorrow; tomorrow will look after itself" (Matt. 6.34), after a number of pictures which he had brought to his followers' attention, showing how God looks after the creatures which he has made. "Each day", he says, "has troubles enough of its own."

The whole context in which these words are spoken strongly implies that over-anxiety about the future is a sign of lack of trust in God our Father. It is one of the results of learning to put our faith in him that we gradually learn to overcome our fears for the future. We are not to suppose, however, that anxieties always disappear at once. Sometimes they are caused by hidden things in our minds of which we do not know the cause, and temptations to anxiety will continue to arise from such causes. But as we grow in the spiritual life, and learn more and more to accept the will of God and to accommodate ourselves to his teaching, these fears will cease to have the hold on us which they had earlier.

As in other aspects of the spiritual life we have to make a distinction between the temptation to anxiety and the giving way to it causing the collapse of a proper faith. The key to dealing with anxiety temptations is to accept them as facts without approving them in the will. Attempts to pretend to ourselves that we have no anxieties merely have the effect of repressing them and driving them into the unconscious whence they will later come forth in order to harry us in some other way. We have to face our fears, to look directly at them, and to accept them in this way. We can then present them to God in our prayer, and with his help begin to exorcize them so as to remove their power.

We have said that there should be a readiness to accept the emotional strains of anxiety while at the same time refusing to it the consent of our will. This is quite different from trying to overcome the anxiety by an act of the will: to do this is to invite worse tensions than those we are trying to cure. So long as we are able in a reasonably calm and coherent frame of mind to offer to God the anxiety and fear which has come upon us, however great may be the suffering which it is causing, we may be confident that we have begun to evacuate it of its power over our souls.

A recent writer, Fr Alan Whittemore, o.h.c., in a pamphlet, *Psychology Reinforced by Religion*, has put it like this:

> For, ultimately, there is only one basis for relaxation which is completely reasonable and therefore effective; namely, the conviction that, behind the multifarious forces which surround us, there is a Being who loves each individual among us with a tender, personal love, and who is competent to protect us. As this conviction grows, and one enters into "the peace of God which passeth all understanding" the obstruction is removed from that interior reservoir of forces, which psychology recognizes but cannot fully release.

These words were written for ordinary people suffering from anxiety. We must recognize that anxiety can come to people even when they have for some time been engaged in living the Christian life. It can come especially in the prayer life: doubts come into the mind when dryness and distraction are predominant, and these can easily sow anxieties about the prayer life itself. Indeed it is one of the most subtle temptations to arouse anxiety under the guise of wanting to do God's will and to go forward in the spiritual life. As we have already seen in the section on calm, this can be most destructive to true prayer, and is to be carefully watched for and guarded against: the advice of a wise director is particularly important in such cases.

It is above all the present with which we are charged to be concerned. What matters is what we are doing with our life now at this very instant. If we ask what the present really is we find that it does not exist in any tangible form. What we usually call the present is the period of time between the not long ago and the not distant future: but strictly speaking this is not the present. The present is the moment of time between all the past and all the future, and when we try to grasp it we find that it is like the geometrical point, it has no magnitude, it does not really exist in isolation, and it cannot be separated from past and future.

Our experience of the present gives us perhaps an inkling of the meaning of eternity, where with God all past and future is one present. In our little way we find ourselves experiencing a present which does not really exist, yet it proves to be the only thing that really matters. We know the present to be inextricably linked with past and future, and know its power to be the determining factor of the future. It is this indescribable thing which we know and which God has given us to use. It is what we do now with our life, with our opportunity, with our attitude that decides the unknown future. If we deal with this insubstantial moment rightly, we find that it solves both past and future, for in it is the seed of eternity itself.

23

Everything is an Opportunity

Everything that happens is an opportunity of serving God and doing his will. This is a fact of the deepest significance and even mystery. In it is found what the redeeming of the world really means in practice. It is at this point that good and evil meet and evil is overcome by good; it is here that sin and love meet, and sin is overcome by love. It is here that suffering as well as evil is conquered, used, transmuted, so as to serve the eternal purpose of God.

As we consider the events of everyday life, it is more and more difficult to explain or to express the truth in a way which is reasonably simple to understand and which at the same time does not distort it. This difficulty is common to all our conversation about spiritual things, but never more so than here.

Perhaps we may sum up the difficulty first by asking a series of questions. Does everything that happens come from God? Am I to think that God himself sends every event which affects me? If so, do I not say that God sends the death of that innocent child, killed by the drunken motorist? And in this case what happens to the idea of a God of love? Some things that happen are evidently the direct result of evil; how then can we say they occur as part of God's will?

Some do not go as far as that, and yet maintain that everything that happens is permitted by God, and therefore has his tacit approval. There is, of course, a *non sequitur* in this sentence. God permits evil in one sense, but it is impossible to say that it has his approval, either tacit or otherwise. He does permit evil, however, because it is an inevitable part of the freedom which he has given to man that man should be able to turn away from God, from the good, and choose what is not good or of God, what is evil. So we may rightly say that God permits evil without approving of it in its expression, because he could only ban it by destroying what he has created, namely free men and women, which would *ex hypothesi* be a greater evil since God can only do what is perfectly good, and it would involve destroying this good.

The evil which we suffer, and which affects us in our everyday life whether in the form of disease or of other people's wickedness, comes from the exercise of free will in defiance of the laws and purposes of God. We must, therefore, absolutely reject the statements, which have been popular in Christian circles at some periods, that evil and suffering come upon us as a direct act of the will of God, either as punishment for our own sins or in order to give us the opportunity of progress by overcoming them. So in the case of illness and disease, we can only say that the will of God is for health, wholeness of body and mind, and that we suffer as part of the rebellion of the created world against God, at the head of which rebellion is man.

Suffering is not to be explained in terms of the individual, but only in terms of the whole creation which has been alienated from the life of God. The solidarity of each man with all mankind is part of the truth of earthly life: it is expressed in the doctrine of original sin and it is daily seen in the sufferings which derive from human evil and which affect individuals without regard to their own particular conscious responsibilities.

We ought, however, to realize that the suffering which we experience in this manner is part of the provision of a beneficent and loving God. The laws of suffering, of health, of safety, of sin and its nemesis, have been incorporated into the world's structure, not to punish men for doing wrong, but in order to lead them to their true interests and to keep them in peace and safety. It is only by the deliberate and constant rejection of the principles which have been built into the universe that the suffering comes.

But having said all this, we have not reached the end. For in the message of the Gospel and above all in the Incarnation of Jesus Christ, the God-Man, we have been brought to a new possibility, a new birth, through which the evil and suffering in the world can be redeemed. I do not intend to equate evil and suffering: evil is always wrong in itself: suffering may derive from something evil but when it comes it is in itself neutral, it is not in itself necessarily wrong. But the attitude in both cases which can bring forth positive life from them is strikingly similar.

Archbishop Nathan Söderblom, a great Swedish theologian, who was a student of comparative religion, pointed out that the attitude of Christianity towards suffering is unique. It does not claim to be able to explain suffering, but it does something immensely more important and harder, it shows the way through suffering to victory. It shows how, first in the cross and afterwards in the lives of Christians, suffering by being embraced can provide victory of a quality and a power which can be found in no other way. That is indeed the essence of the Christian claim about suffering and the results of evil: for those who can accept them and use them in Christ they are the shortest way to God.

An evil act must here be distinguished from the results of an evil act. No evil act in itself can be anything but a betrayal of God and of the teaching of Jesus. It is in itself a deliberate act of rebellion and as such brings immense harm, not only to the person who does it but to the human race generally, for it adds to the mounting pressure of evil with which man must wrestle. But the consequences of an evil act can be redeemed. In short, God can and does bring good out of evil. The outstanding example is of course the cross, an act as evil as any that has ever been perpetrated, yet it is out of this evil that our redemption has been wrought. So God can bring good out of every evil in the lives of all those who are incorporated into Christ and share with him his saving victory.

The simplest example is perhaps that of our own sin. Our sinful act is an act of rebellion, but, as soon as it is recognized as such and is repented of, God can use it to advance us in the way of our salvation. He can cause it to increase our own virtues, such as humility, and our reliance on God alone instead of on our own strength: he can use it to increase our determination in the future and to show us truths which we had not known before: he can in fact give us more abounding grace. But we must then echo

St Paul's words and reject with horror the idea that we should sin in order that grace should abound. Such an idea is a contradiction in terms.

So we see how everything that happens is an opportunity of serving God. Even our own past sins and the sins of others, once they have taken place, are opportunities for serving God and coming nearer to him through his help and guidance. Once this truth has penetrated to the inmost recesses of our souls, we see that we can only use such opportunities when we accept them as such. If we rebel against what occurs, we set up in our own souls a rejection of the opportunity, and thus make it impossible for us to use it as God wants. We may also very easily set up other psychological or emotional tensions, which make our spiritual growth much more difficult.

In our daily life, therefore, we should see each event which we meet as an opportunity for drawing nearer to God, for seeking his will, and for trying to follow his guiding. In this way we are united to Christ and may join with him in redeeming the sin and suffering of the world, if one may so put it. It is in this way that we see how we as members of the Church are indeed joined with Christ in the work of redemption, which was begun on the cross and is made actual through his body the Church until the work is ready for the final consummation of all things.

From the practical point of view it is how we deal with the present moment that matters. It was, I think, Fr J. P. de Caussade who invented the illuminating phrase "the sacrament of the present moment". It is a phrase which contains a wealth of meaning and a wealth of truth, namely that God is to be found in each present moment by the soul who seeks him there, and who accepts each event of each moment as an opening for doing his will and finding his grace. This not only implies a particular approach to each present moment, but also puts the past and the future in their right perspectives. "One must restrict oneself to the present duty without thinking of the preceding one, or of the one which is to follow", and: "In the state of abandonment the only rule is the duty of the present moment."[1]

[1] *Abandonment to Divine Providence*, bk ii, ch. 2, sec. 6.

It is true that Fr de Caussade is writing of a whole area of spiritual development which we are not discussing now, but there is no doubt that the principle which is here emphasized is a key to all aspects of the life of prayer and of the Christian life which lead to closer union with God through Jesus Christ. Each moment provides us with the raw material for serving God. Whatever it is, whatever its origin, Christ asks us to join with him in taking it, redeeming it, and making it powerful in our own lives and in the world for the building up of his kingdom.

24

In his Service is Freedom and Joy

The Anglican Book of Common Prayer uses the phrase "whose service is perfect freedom" and in doing so points to one of the secrets of the life of prayer and the Christian life. In explaining the Christian life to those who do not know it a constant difficulty is found in the fact that terms in common use have a different meaning for the two parties taking part in the conversation. The worldly use of the word "freedom" is far removed from that of the Christian, though there is something in common between them. The reason is simple. For the man of the world freedom refers to outward things, which affect his worldly standing and activities: for the Christian the word refers to spiritual forces from which he has been freed, or is in process of being freed by the grace of God.

Basically the two meanings can be reduced on the one hand to "freedom from restrictions on my own will" and on the other "freedom from the power of sin". Both do refer to restriction in some sense, but otherwise they are poles apart. That is why such a phrase "whose service is perfect freedom" can only fully make sense to one who has some experience or understanding of the Christian message, and what it means in the life of the individual Christian.

The freedom of God is the only true freedom, because it is the only means by which the powers of the personality can be released and can fully flower. Man has been made to love God and to live in him: it is only when this purpose begins to be fulfilled that he becomes free from the restraints which sin and other shortcomings of his personality exercise over his development. When this restraint goes, an experience of freedom quite different from any other comes to be known.

Christian freedom is compatible with outward constraint. It can be known in the worst of material circumstances—in prison, in illness, in poverty, and in loneliness. Indeed it is often the case, as we have seen elsewhere, that adverse outward circumstances are the very means by which the inner freedom is acquired, for a new depth of serving God is found by his grace in such circumstances, and thus the new kind of freedom is experienced.

Christ himself was the most truly free of all men, being perfect man in every facet of his character and human personality. Yet he was incapable of sin. This to some seems to be a contradiction, because they see freedom primarily as a matter of choice, either to do good or to do evil, either to obey God or to disobey him. But this is a false approach to the matter since, so long as a man is able to turn from God he cannot be free, for he is still subject to the pressure of sin to such an extent as to be able to reject God, and in rejecting God to reject freedom in its deepest meaning. The man who is fully free has escaped altogether from the power of sin and sin has no possibility of enticing him away from God. There is, therefore, at the deepest spiritual level a paradox, that the man who is truly free is the man who has no other choice than to serve God.

St Augustine puts the matter with his usual clarity and incisiveness:

> The souls in bliss will possess the freedom of the will, though sin will have no power to tempt them. They will be more free than ever—so free, in fact, from all delight in sinning as to find, in not sinning, an unfailing source of joy. By the freedom which was given to the first man, who was constituted in rectitude, he could choose either to sin or not to sin; in eternity, freedom is that more potent freedom which makes all sin impossible. Such freedom, of course, is a gift of God, beyond the power of nature to achieve.[1]

In this passage St Augustine links freedom with joy. The two cannot indeed be separated, since both are the result of fulfilment according to the will of God. But here again the word "joy" when used by Christians has a different and a deeper meaning than its normal use in the world. It speaks of spiritual experience

[1] *City of God*, bk 22, ch. 30, p. 541.

which is independent of outward trouble and hardship: it reflects communion with God which is often found only through suffering, which, strangely enough, is far from incompatible with joy, but is often united with it and produces a deeper realization of spiritual joy than could otherwise be known.

"Joy" is a wonderful word whose full meaning is only to be found in the Christian life. Other names are used for various aspects of this experience, such as "the peace of God which passeth all understanding" and similar expressions. They are feeble attempts to touch a reality which far surpasses the power of human words because it springs directly from contact with the life of God himself. It is something beyond the feelings as they are usually understood, though if we are asked to describe more exactly what this joy is like, it is difficult to do so without some use of the word "feeling". It is different from other experiences for it transcends them, it is above or below them, according to the language which seems most appropriate. It is at the deepest level of human love, and, being spiritual, cannot be captured in any adequate description. Only a poet or a musician can touch its fringes.

25

Sins and Virtues

It would be difficult to deny that sins and virtues are important, yet they are commonly given far more importance than they ought to have. Perhaps in our modern world the stress that is put on practical things encourages this. It is the man that produces results who is admired. This is part of the reign of applied science in our world, and the adulation which is showered on those who succeed in such adventures as sending a man to the moon encourages this mental attitude.

But, it might be said, is not this in accord with the New Testament, in which we have the words of our Lord that men shall be tested by the fruits which they produce, and in other places that it is their actions which will determine whether they will be received into the presence of God or be cast into outer darkness? The parable of the sheep and the goats brings out this aspect of the teaching of Jesus in a powerful way. "Inasmuch as ye have done it unto one of the least of these my brethren, ye have done it unto me" (Matt. 25.40), or in the New English Bible: "Anything you did for one of my brothers here, however humble, you did for me." It would be absurd to deny the importance which we find in the Gospels and in other parts of the New Testament attached to sins and virtues in the sense of practical actions.

Indeed, as we have seen elsewhere, actions are the practical expressions of the will, which remains at the centre of the human personality and of the spiritual life. Yet, in spite of all this—perhaps it would be more accurate to say because of it—too much attention focused on sins and virtuous actions can and often does have the wrong result, for it turns the direction of life in a legalistic direction, and concentrates attention on outward things instead of on the inward reality.

For side by side with the stress on the importance of outward actions which we have just mentioned, we find a parallel and almost opposite stress on the all important character of inward attitudes. The Sermon on the Mount is the oustanding example of this, where Jesus tries to teach his hearers that it is the heart which is the determining factor of all else. The Beatitudes speak of the inner character, not of outward works: they speak of the blessings which belong to those who know they are poor, who are sorrowful, gentle, who hunger and thirst after right, who show mercy, are pure in heart, are peacemakers, and who suffer persecution for the right. These are not descriptions of outward achievements but of inward character.

In prayer it is above all this inward quality which is of the utmost importance, and too much thought about sins and virtuous actions can and often does lead away from our contact with God into all kinds of distracting considerations. We do not mean that our prayer rejects good works—far from it. Our prayer life is the means, one could say the only means, by which good works can properly come in the right relation to God and with reliance on his grace. Good works are not the purpose of our prayer, but the inevitable result of a spiritual life truly aligned with the will of God.

So with our sins—they are the result of a state of sinfulness, and can only be overcome by the gradual transformation of the state of sinfulness through the power of God acting in our life, through our prayer, and through our constant and regular participation in the sacraments. To spend time in our prayer considering detailed sins is almost always wrong beyond the point when it is necessary to recall them shortly, in order to confess them.

All is to be seen in relation to love, which is of course the only standard of our life of prayer. It is by learning more and more the nature of the love of God, by entering into it and submitting to it, by hearing its voice and receiving its strength, that our lives become what God wants them to be. As love grows, sins and virtuous actions are seen in their right proportion as temporary expressions of the failure or success of God's work in the soul. They can be used to teach us humility and thanksgiving and thus promote the glory of God, and assist our own growth through his goodness.

We come back as always to the basic facts of the life of prayer, namely that it is to be concentrated on God to the utmost extent which our strength and his grace permits, for here is the beginning, continuation, and end of all spiritual things—to grow according to God's will in his love.

26

All comes from God

It is in prayer that the paradoxes which we find in ordinary human logic are overcome. They do not cease to exist, but they are seen to be held together in a mysterious unity which is greater than the seeming contradictions of human logic. Such a statement sounds as if it were the beginning of an attempt to justify the abolition of reason in favour of intuition, or of some individualistic inspirationalism which will make reason out of date. Nothing could be further from the truth. Reason is the power given by God, to which men must continue to be faithful without compromise.

But in prayer the limits of reason are quickly reached. We come to a point beyond which reason does not help us to proceed. Even if we think of ordinary human personal relations, something of the same limitations are easily perceived, for example in the growth of the deeper relationship of love between human beings. It is not that reason is discarded, but that it is transcended.

Prayer especially brings us quickly to the boundaries of the area where reason can enlighten us. In order to state the deep truths of the spiritual life, seemingly contradictory statements have to be made in order to do anything like justice to the truth of experience. If we state that all comes from God we must contradict it by saying that God is not the author of evil, and that sin is the very opposite of God—turning away from him. Nevertheless when all that side has been set down it remains a deep spiritual truth that everything that happens is an expression of what God permits: in some unexplained and inexplicable sense even our sins are within the total framework of existence, which only remains in existence because it is the will of the God, in whom resides all being, that it should be so.

So too, as we have seen, every occurrence in our lives, whether outward or inward, whether the effect of other forces upon us or the apparent haphazard development of our spiritual life, everything is an opportunity for serving God. This means that we can use each event for the glory of God. Yes, but it is deeper than that. God is somehow to be found within the event. De Caussade's expression, "the sacrament of the present moment", means more, and rightly means more, than that we can juggle with each event in some useful way; it means that each event has a mysterious content which in some way is connected with God. God cannot be shaken off. As the psalmist sang: "Whither shall I go then from thy Spirit: or whither shall I go then from thy presence? If I climb up into heaven thou are there: if I go down to hell, thou art there also." (Ps. 139.6f.)

There are other seeming contradictions which lose their force in the life of prayer. Grace and free will, faith and works, predestination and personal freedom, these and others are solved on a deeper plane than the merely rational. Life is greater than any one aspect of it and all our faculties together are not enough to do more than illuminate one small area of the infinite and endless variety and truth which is God.

In the prayer life the knowledge that all comes from God, that everything that happens, even when it is from an evil source, is somehow within the providence of the God who is Almighty in love and power is a guiding principle of immense import. It means in practice that we need never have any fears about our prayer when we do our part to the best of our ability, for we launch ourselves in our little ship of prayer on the great ocean of the love of God, which will inevitably and surely bring us home to the port, where it is his will that we should haven.

Sometimes we are tempted to think we have been deserted by the love of God in our prayer. Such ideas are temptations to make us abandon ship and give up—the only action which can thwart the intention of God for us. For whatever evil temptations or trials may assail us, we may be confident that the free out-flowing love and grace of God far surpasses anything which the enemy can bring against us, and that if we only have faith, he will give us blessings beyond anything which we can ever think or desire.

27

Blankness and Darkness

There are few who try seriously to make prayer the centre of their lives who are not assailed by the difficulties of blankness and darkness. As to the first, it is a common form of trial and must be faced frankly by those who are determined to follow the path of the will of God. It is also called dryness, though there is some difference between them. Dryness may describe merely the absence of any pleasurable emotion or experience in prayer, and it may be particularly difficult to bear after spiritual enjoyments have been known. This is the first stage on the way of weaning the soul from going to prayer for its delights instead of as a means of learning and submitting to the will of God. Dryness is a sign of progress in the life of prayer, though it is widely mistaken for a sign of regress.

It must always be understood, therefore, that periods of dryness are to be expected, and indeed that the training and progress of the soul, so far as it can be judged from what we learn by experience, necessitates these periods, which can be prolonged for many months or years. But all the time in them God is helping the soul to grow stronger, and to strengthen its wings by making it rely exclusively on God's call to the will and not on his gifts of pleasant feelings.

Blankness is more than dryness and includes the absence of any kind of coherent content in the prayer. Meditation becomes barren and impossible, and there seems to be no useful activity going on at all during the time of prayer. It is more than the absence of agreeable feelings—it is the absence of all that we normally think of as prayer, so far as it can be described. Such experiences are severe trials, for they immensely strengthen the natural temptation to give up times of prayer, where nothing at all seems to happen in spite of all attempts to find a remedy. Yet there is no doubt that this experience too plays its part in the strengthening of the weak parts of the spiritual personality, preparing it for whatever future God has in store for it.

It is important to understand that such experiences can go on for a very long time, and it is not for us to dictate to God the extent of them. He alone can guide the spirit aright and it must be humbly accepted with faith and submission. It is good in these circumstances to give up trying to make any formal prayer, but rather to continue to make acts of love and submission, praying God all the time to accomplish his will and to strengthen faith. What would be quite fatal would be to think that it would be good to give prayer a rest for a time, with the intention of coming back to it with a fresh outlook. Such a course can lead to nothing but disaster: it weakens the will, encourages a false idea of what prayer is for, and breaks up the pattern of the spiritual life, which may have been established only after long and arduous work.

As to darkness, this is yet a further stage of trial, where God seems to be withdrawing himself from the person concerned. We cannot speak of the fearful trials of darkness which the great saints of prayer have undergone, but we can see that even in the early stages of the ascent of the soul to God experiences of darkness are known to some degree. The remedy is of course the same. Indeed one could say that there is only one remedy for all the troubles and trials of the prayer life, namely to continue to trust in God that he is leading the soul and training it in the way he wants, and never to cease to give to him as an act of humble love the time of prayer which alone is the earnest of our desire to do his will.

St Paul compared himself to a man in a race. We may follow him in noticing how hard and how seriously the athlete must prepare himself in mind and body, if he is to be the victor. How much more is training needed for the athlete of God. Training always involves hard and dull patches, but it is obvious to anyone who looks that it is these very times which are most productive in producing in the athlete the self-control and directed energy which he needs for his task. Is there then any cause for surprise when we find that God takes the training of his athletes seriously and makes them go through the hardships, which are the indispensable preliminaries for victory?

28

Unity

The life of prayer is growth in unity with God. And because it is this it is also growth in unity with all our fellow Christians who are likewise growing nearer to God in their prayer. The twentieth century has seen a wonderful increase among Christians in the desire for unity: they have been more and more seized with a sense of sin for the appalling denials of God's love, of which they and their Churches are guilty. We must all thank God for this new awareness.

One result has been that many Christian leaders have been engaged in the practical work of trying to remedy the divisions among themselves. They have studied their theological differences in the Faith and Order Movement and elsewhere, they have worked together in joint projects in the Life and Work Movement (both now within the World Council of Churches); they have formed mergers between traditionally similar bodies; they have made new schemes and plans to bring different traditions together. All this is welcome evidence of a new sense of responsibility to the unity for which Christ lived and died.

But there is an evident gap on the deepest level of all—that of prayer. Here there are, thank God, new stirrings too, especially in the prayer now found all over the world during the week of prayer for Christian unity each year from 18 to 25 January. And that saintly Roman Catholic priest, the Abbé Paul Couturier, taught many Christians inside and outside his own Church the true spirit of Christ in which prayer for unity should be approached: it needs still to grow.

Yet surely in the long run it is only in praying for union with God himself that each of us can truly contribute to Christian unity, because only in God himself can any unity have a basis which will endure because it is in accordance with his will. Working together, discussing theological questions together, joining church organizations together, even praying for unity among Christians are all in a sense secondary, for none of them can be rightly done unless our spirits are first of all conformed, as wholly as they can be, to the will of God.

Moreover, it is in a new appreciation and understanding of one another's spirituality that we touch the deepest and most important aspects of our Christian lives. We must learn from each other how to pray one another's prayers, so that our prayers become one, united in what is common and vivifying. There are differences in approaches to prayer in different parts of Christendom, and these must be recognized. But they are mostly concerned with matters which are not of the deepest importance. And we find that the differences are mainly found in one of two aspects. Either in the theories about the nature of prayer, or in those parts of prayer which deal with the more elementary and less deep stages. In the first of these two aspects it is clear that theorizing about prayer will always lead to differences, merely because we are trying to comprehend in the feeble forms of human words experiences which themselves are beyond words, and more than that, endeavouring to imprison the plans of God for the spiritual lives of men in a tidy scheme which will be small enough to be understood by human minds. Such attempts are bound to fail.

In the second aspect there is no doubt that, where Christians are deeply committed to the life of prayer, they find themselves in remarkable agreement on matters of importance. It is here in the depths of the spiritual life, where words are no longer useful instruments, that we must seek the unity which transcends our barriers, and draw from the fount of God himself that strength and that spiritual sight and understanding, which will once more release spiritual power to overcome our sins, our prejudices, our ignorances, and our malice.

There seems little reason to doubt that, if Christendom would for a time abandon its outward activities, many of them excellent, and concentrate on more and deeper prayer, many things, which appear as problems now, would take on another appearance. For in this way we should be more able to give free reign to the power of the Holy Spirit, that rushing mighty wind, who alone can sweep away the cobwebs and dirt of our hearts, filling them with the breath of God himself.

APPENDIX

Quietism

The place of calm in the life of prayer can hardly be considered without some attention being given to the question of Quietism, and the condemnation of this doctrine in the West, and the traces of it in the East. In the Eastern Orthodox tradition "Hesychasm" is an exact translation in Greek of the word "Quietism", but it does not carry the same technical meaning. In the West the word has come to describe those particular negative doctrines of self-abnegation and quiet which have been condemned by ecclesiastical authority. It is, therefore, somewhat meaningless to ask whether quietism ought to have been condemned, if the word is restricted to the doctrines which were in fact condemned. For there can be little doubt that in the extreme form in which they were condemned their condemnation was just.

It is another question to ask whether those who were condemned as holding these doctrines were justly censured. Some have held that Molinos was not a quietist, although he is generally held to be the first exponent of the doctrine to which the name was applied, just as some hold that Nestorius was not a Nestorian, or Pelagius a Pelagian. Perhaps it is not necessary to inquire at this stage whether the condemnation of Molinos and others was just, Fénelon and Mme Guyon among them. It is important, however, to see where teaching did and could go astray and what is the right attitude to the issues at stake. For it cannot be denied that the debate about quietism did deal with issues of importance.

One difficulty in the matter is that the dividing line between what is permissible and what is heretical is difficult to trace with any exactness. In dealing with states of prayer, language is always inexact, for it is never more than approximately accurate in describing spiritual attitudes and conditions. When, therefore, one is trying to draw a line between the state of calm or quiet which is an essential element in a well-balanced spiritual attitude and a state of quietism which is the abandonment of a proper attitude, there is apt to be confusion.

In the Eastern Orthodox tradition the discussion seems never to have been conducted with the same definition as in the West. This is not to be wondered at, for the West is far more prone to categorization than the Orthodox East. Some confusion is caused by the varying meanings given to the word "Hesychasm" by Orthodox writers. Several causes can be found for this. In the first place, as hesychasm has played an important part at various times, Orthodox writers are not prepared to criticize it adversely if it can be avoided. This is one of the results of a strong but undefined sense of tradition: it results in an attitude of mind which accepts things which have been present for a long time without critical examination, with the seeming implication that as they have existed for a long time and have been looked upon with veneration by many Orthodox people and through many centuries, therefore they must be part of the "Holy Tradition", which cannot be questioned without impiety. But such an attitude as this often prevents a proper detachment of mind and results in an impoverishment of learning, for God surely teaches his people by their mistakes as well as by achievements.

In the Orthodox use of the word, hesychasm is used to cover writers as far apart as Evagrius (346–99) and St Gregory Palamas (1296–1359). By some writers hesychasm seems almost to be equated with the use of the Jesus Prayer, as for example by Vladimir Lossky in his *Mystical Theology of the Eastern Church* (pp. 209ff; English ed.). In others it seems to describe the eremitical (individual hermits) as opposed to the coenobitic (community) life of monks, as for example when Basil Krivosheine writes: "It may be said in general that when the community spirit developed at the expense of the hesychastic (owing largely to the growth of big monasteries) this led to a weakening of the inner force of monasticism and to its attraction to outward, often purely economic forms of activity."[1] Elsewhere it is thought to describe some particular technique of prayer and contemplation, sometimes the method of physical posture, etc., rather like *yoga*, sometimes some other elaborate technique of prayer and meditation.[2]

It is clear from all this that hesychasm as a term needs much more clarification than it has received up to the present, and a good deal more agreement is needed among Orthodox exponents of their own tradition. But it also becomes clear that the word evidently does not correspond with the Western word "Quietism", although, as we shall see, there is much in common in the problems with which both are attempting to deal.

Another point which ought to be noted is the use of words among the earlier mystical and ascetical writers which had close affinities to those in use among the Stoics and Platonists from whom the Quietists derive the main doctrines for which they were condemned. In particular the Greek words apatheia ($\dot{\alpha}\pi\dot{\alpha}\theta\epsilon\iota\alpha$) and ataraxia ($\dot{\alpha}\tau\alpha\rho\alpha\xi\dot{\iota}\alpha$) with their translations can lead to much confusion. They may be translated passionlessness, or dispassion, or sometimes calmness or quiet. But they have been understood in different senses, and it is in the understanding of them that the division between quietism and sound doctrine is to be found.

Hesychasm is also identified with the views of Gregory Palamas in his controversy with Barlaam the Calabrian on the subject of the uncreated light of God and his energies. This aspect of the matter, which is more theoretical than practical, so far as the life of prayer is concerned, need not be examined now. In its origin the controversy was closely connected with methods of prayer which were alleged to produce the ineffable joy of seeing the divine light, identified with the supernatural light which surrounded our Lord at his transfiguration on Mount Tabor. The light in question was held to be uncreated and available to the senses, though distinct from the very essence of the Godhead. This theory was eventually generally accepted in the Orthodox world

[1] *Eastern Churches Quarterly*, 1938, No. 4, p. 52.
[2] Cf. *St John Climacus*, Introduction by M. Heppill, p. 26.

of the fourteenth century, but like many other subjects was entangled in political and ecclesiastical intrigues in the course of its discussion.

The serious element for the life of prayer is the spread of the idea that the vision of God could be obtained by the adoption of the right technique, a theory which is totally heretical in all circumstances wherever it appears. It is heretical for the very simple reason that it denies the basis of Christian Faith, namely that the spiritual life is a growth of relationship between a human person and the God who is love, and can only be understood or interpreted in that sense. It is a contradiction in terms to maintain that the growth of a relationship of love can be achieved by mere technique.

Even to-day some enthusiasts for the Jesus Prayer, especially among the Russian Orthodox and their admirers, use language about it which may suggest that it is a technique which itself produces a state of prayer and union with God. An article published in 1960 in a Church paper about the Jesus Prayer was entitled "The Greatest Prayer of All", an example of the absurd lengths to which unbridled enthusiasm can go, without any attempt to relate it to the New Testament or to the teaching of our Lord. No one would wish to deny that the use of this method of prayer has been and can be of great help to many people: but it is not the answer to all difficulties of the spiritual life!

But let us return for a moment to the pre-Christian conception of *apatheia* (apathy or passionlessness) which undoubtedly has a continuous life from the doctrine of some of the Fathers to that of later Quietists. The importance of entire escape from the emotions is found in the Stoics, though the history of the idea is older than that. Plato himself opposed the stoic conception of apathy, but the idea was revived in various teachers and is found again rather strongly in later Philosophy and in Neo-Platonism whence it was brought in to the teaching of Christian spirituality.[1] It was much encouraged by the teaching of the Neo-Platonists about the *via negativa* and is said to have taken an Asiatic rather than a Greek form since the time of Dionysius the Pseudo-

[1] *Encyclopaedia of Religion and Ethics*, vol. 1, p. 604.

Areopagite, whose influence was so immense on the development of schools of Christian prayer.[1] Both in the West and in the East his writings enjoyed a position of apostolic authority for many centuries.

Dionysius is now known to have lived at about the beginning of the sixth century and to have had no connection with the Dionysius who is mentioned in the New Testament. But the teaching of *apatheia* circulated and similar ideas are found strongly put forward by Evagrius during the fourth century in a form which also had considerable influence, especially in the East. His teaching has been summed up as follows:

This theory of the ascetic life as a stripping of the soul finds its most notable presentation in Evagrius's doctrine of gnosis and prayer. The highest state of gnosis consists in *theologia*, which is knowledge of the Holy Trinity filling the mind (*nous*), a condition identical with his most characteristic phrase, the state of "pure prayer" (καθαρὰ προσευχή). Pure prayer does not only mean prayer separated from sin. The purity of the prayer must be judged from its intellectual as well as its moral aspects. Since God is simple and infinite being, the mind will be unable to approach him so long as it remains complex, i.e. burdened with wandering thoughts, with spiritual images, or with intellectual concepts. Prayer is the lifting up of the mind to God [Evagrius is the author of this famous definition]: but the mind cannot attain to him unless it is stripped naked (γυμνός, ψιλός, κωφός, ἄλαλος). Hence not merely evil thoughts hinder pure prayer, but *all thoughts*. Evagrius can define prayer as "the expulsion of thoughts". The highest part of the soul must be deprived first of its passions, then of its thoughts and its images; yet it is not left in vacuity, for in its pure state it becomes filled with God, with the light of the Holy Trinity so that it shines like some sparkling sapphire. *Nous* has become the temple of the Holy Trinity. In such gnosis the mind loses self-consciousness and attains to a condition named by Evagrius *anaesthesia*, which corresponds to the spiritual ecstasy of later writers.[2]

The similarity of this exposition to the teaching of the Quietists of the seventeenth century is very striking. It is plain that there is a thread running from the pagan Greek teaching, perhaps

[1] Op. cit., vol. x, p. 534.
[2] Owen Chadwick, *John Cassian*, pp. 84f.

affected by Asiatic influences at a later date, through the Neo-Platonists and such teachers as Evagrius, to the Hesychasts in the East and the Quietists in the West. But, of course, not all who learnt from these teachers adopted the exaggerations of which we have spoken. Many of them learnt important truths which were set in relation to the teaching of the Gospels, and thus were made to serve true Christian spirituality rather than to distract from it.

So far as the influence of Evagrius on Eastern thought is concerned, his views were not allowed to exist without correction, and Gregory Palamas himself was at pains to correct their exaggerations. It is true that with Origen Evagrius was condemned at the Fifth Oecumenical Council (553), but this did not prevent his influence from being widespread. Dr Jean Meyendorff has written:

The "discovery" of Evagrius as the common father of the Eastern Christian mystics, however, poses a historical and dogmatic problem of the greatest importance. Is not the deacon of Pontus a heretic condemned, as Origen was, for his platonic spiritualism at the 5th Oecumenical Council? But while the "doctrines of Origen"—about which one cannot always know whether they do in fact stem from Origen—have been, at least in part, corrected by the Cappadocians or by St Maximus, the teaching of Evagrius penetrated clandestinely, in its original form and under the imprint of St Nilus, into the most venerable patristic tradition! It is true that these works of the Pontian, of which we find quotations in almost all the Greek spiritual authors up to and including Palamas, do not contain materially the "Origenic" errors condemned under Justinian; but it is not less true that the purely intellectualist mysticism of Evagrius, such as we find for example in the *De Oratione*, faithfully reflects neoplatonist spirituality, with almost no corrective; some sparse references to the Word and to the Trinity certainly reveal a Christian author, but it is enough to state that in this work there is *no* reference to the Incarnation as such, still less to the Church and sacraments, and that prayer is essentially conceived as an immaterial contact of the intelligence with God (ἄϋλος τῷ ἀύλῳ πρόσιθι, 66) as a "prelude to immaterial knowledge" (προΐμιον τῆς ἀύλου γνώσεως, 85) so that the Incarnation *cannot* have any place in the philosophy of existence and the spirituality which these lines reveal.[1]

[1] *Introduction à l'Étude de Grégoire Palamas*, pp. 196f.

Dr Meyendorff goes on to point out that although the vocabulary of Evagrius became permanently accepted in the Eastern Church, his ideas underwent a clear correction of a christological kind, especially at the hands of St Maximus the Confessor. Later Barlaam the Calabrian was a supporter of the essential principles of a platonist anthropology and this lay at the bottom of Gregory Palamas's opposition to him. The task of Palamas in defending hesychasm was not easy in the light of the abuses to which psycho-physical methods of prayer had led. Dr Meyendorff considers that non-Christian influence in this field is more likely to have come from Mohammedan *dhikr* than from Hindu *yoga*, but from whichever source these practices originated, they clearly upset the balance of Christian understanding of the method and aim of the spiritual life.

From this extremely short and inadequate survey we can see clearly enough that in Christian practice conceptions and methods which were not Christian, and in certain important respects opposed to the revelation of the Gospel, are to be found in Christian tradition. It might be thought that these are not particularly relevant to the twentieth century, but in fact the recent revival of interest in the spiritual life and in all kinds of mysticism, well exemplified by the books of Aldous Huxley on the subject, has brought with it a complete confusion as to the teaching of Christianity about the spiritual life, and it tends to spread the dangerous idea that all attempts at mysticism or the life of prayer are really the same thing, and that it does not matter whether a man is a Hindu mystic, a Buddhist, a Muslim, or a Christian, that there is no fundamental difference between them, that they are all merely methods of attaining the mystical state which is within the reach of anyone who can devote himself seriously enough to mastering the methods of reaching it.

The answer to this is that the teaching of Christianity about the prayer life is totally different from that of the non-Christian religions of the East, even if those other religions have in fact understood some truths and ideas which are useful in the right context. For the Christian Faith is concerned with love between God and man, a relationship which is essentially personal in its proper sense, and which retains the individual distinction between the two and does not teach the absorption of the human into the divine. Archbishop Söderblom of Sweden was right when he said that the authentic note of Judaism and Christianity in the relations between God and man is a meeting of distinct personal entities, neither of which is absorbed in the other.

Quietism, properly speaking, denies this personal relationship by abolishing everything which makes for personal identity, and thus approximates to the impersonal God of non-Christian religion: above all it cuts itself off from the Incarnation and all that that doctrine implies. Nevertheless some, if not all, of those who have been accused of quietism have written much of great value in their spiritual writings. The accusation against them does not chiefly lie in their failure to perceive many true things about the spiritual life, but in the lack of proportion which has led to an extreme view which is not in accordance with true Christian teaching.

There is a true teaching of quiet in the mystical life which is found in the best exponents of the spiritual life such as St Teresa of Avila or St John of the Cross and many others. It is not against such teaching that the condemnation was directed, but against divagations from it. Though Fénelon in defending Mme Guyon found himself condemned not only by Bossuet, his chief opponent, but by the Church, for some of his statements, yet there can be no doubt that much of his spiritual writing is of the highest value, exhibiting great spiritual insight, and that it has proved of help to many who have tried to follow the way of prayer.

In an admirable summary of these negative tendencies in Christian mysticism W. R. Inge wrote that he regarded the *via negativa* of which they formed a part in metaphysics, religion, and ethics "as the great accident of Christian mysticism".[1] But he goes on to say that the negative road is not all error: it does correspond to an important negative side of religion and to the limitations of the finite when compared to the infinite, the limitations of man face to face with God.

[1] *Christian Mysticism*, p. 115.

Extracts from Spiritual Writers

Extracts from Spiritual Writers

The following extracts are taken from spiritual literature of many lands and centuries. The selection is not governed by any particular plan, but merely by the principle of including those passages of ancient and modern authors which have seemed to the compiler to say something illuminating and helpful for the practical life of prayer. No attempt has been made to represent the complete views of each author by this method: any such attempt would be doomed to failure before it began. The amount of literature on the spiritual life is so immense and varied that it would be necessary to write a book on each teacher in order to explain his views. There is no substitute for reading the author himself as a means of finding out what he taught, and short cuts are to be deprecated, though, of course, commentators are of great assistance and often indispensable.

Even in such a limited selection as that which follows some of the difficulties of the subject will appear. It would be oversimplification to suggest that all writers on the spiritual life teach exactly the same thing. Like other authors in their writing they reflect the intellectual and spiritual atmosphere of their time. They speak in the language which it was customary to use, and they use the ideas which were current coin among their contemporaries. There are also wide differences in the way in which writers use the same words—"contemplation" is a case in point, and covers a wide range of different experiences, for which allowance must be made.

But in spite of all these differences there is a remarkable unity underneath, and this is only what one would expect where the spiritual life is being discussed. Where writers are describing the experience of growing in closeness with God, there is bound to be a basic agreement about it, a unity which cannot be lost, where that growth is genuine. On the other hand, God is so much greater than the greatest of human beings—infinitely greater indeed—that no teacher can claim to have an exclusive knowledge of what union with God entails spiritually. Each can claim the authenticity of his own experience so far as it goes, but it does not alter the fact that every other person in the world may have a different experience, because (*a*) God is infinite and may show to each other person a different facet of his life and truth, and (*b*) men are as various as their numbers, and each is different from every other, and therefore sees everything slightly differently from everyone else.

If we take various schools of devotion we may mark immense variety between, shall we say, the desert Fathers and the spiritual writings of eighteenth-century England. Whereas in the former we find the main emphasis on passionlessness (*apatheia*), in the latter much stress seems often to be on the emotions. Yet when one penetrates beneath the surface and asks, for example, what the latter teach when they are finding dryness and difficulty in their prayer, and when emotions seem to have fled, we find that they too teach something very close to the main stream which is to be found in every century and place.

There are, too, modern writers of particular brilliance and depth whom we should do well to study. Some of them are mentioned in the list of authors: there are doubtless many more who might have been included, but a limit has to be chosen, and this will always be to a certain extent arbitrary, governed by the preferences and reading of the selector. The present author can only hope that some of the selections will prove to be as helpful to those who read them as they have been to him.

MORTIFICATION

ST IGNATIUS OF LOYOLA

[*On exterior penance*]

The first is in regard to food. Here it is necessary to remark that when we cut off what is superfluous this is not penance but temperance. It becomes penance when we retrench from what is suitable, and the more we retrench, the greater and the better is the penance, provided only health is not injured, and no notable infirmity ensues.

The Spiritual Exercises of St Ignatius of Loyola, tr. and ed. by W. H. Longridge, S.S.J.E., p. 73.

AUGUSTINE BAKER

[Note on mortification]

1 Quietly to suffer all crosses, difficulties and contradictions to self-will whether internal or external, including temptations and dryness. This is the very essence of a mortified life.

2 Never to do or omit things on account of one's likes and dislikes, but refer all to God's will.

3 Those mortifications are right for us which increase humility and power of prayer and are performed with cheerful resolution. They are wrong, if deliberately undertaken instead of the obvious difficulties of life and if they produce depression and strain.

4 Habitual quietness of mind is essential to true mortification. All impetuosity and unquietness has in it some self-love but the Holy Spirit is stillness, serenity and peace.

5 In general, the mortifications sent by God and the ordinary friction of existence are enough to discipline our souls. Voluntary mortifications are *never* to be assumed till the necessary difficulties and contradictions of life are cheerfully and fully accepted.

The Letters of Evelyn Underhill, p. 193.

EVELYN UNDERHILL

As to self-abnegation: be ready to accept every mortification and sacrifice God asks of you in unruffled peace—but No Cross-Hunting! Your consecration means tranquil abiding in love with Christ, through ups and downs and lights and darknesses—just as they come, without self-will, doesn't it? But requests for yet another dose of powder without jam, are only inverted self-will! *Far* the best way to deal with self-love, is to let it die of starvation because you are wholly concentrated on His love, within which you can safely love all things, from your dog to the Seraphim, can't you?

Ibid., p. 326.

JEAN PIERRE CAMUS

Our dear Saint [St Francis de Sales] disapproved of immoderate fasting. He used to say that the spirit could not endure the body when over-fed, but that if under-fed, the body could not endure the spirit. He advised judicious treatment of both, saying that God likes to be served with judgment; it is easy to lower the body if necessary, but it is not always easy to restore strength which has been injudiciously wasted. It is easier to wound than to heal. The spirit ought to treat the body as its child, when obedient, and not overwhelm it; but if it revolts, it must be treated as a rebellious subject, even as St Paul says "I chastise my body, and keep it under." If it behaves as a brute it must be treated with whip and bridle, like "our brother the ass", as St Francis of Assisi said.

The Spirit of St Francis de Sales, p. 191.

HARRIET MONSELL

As regards fasting, do what you can in simple ways. Fix on three definite acts of self-denial—one as regards food, one as regards words, one as regards habits of self-indulgence, and watch carefully about these points, being very faithful to your resolve. Try little things, not great things. Little things very faithfully done will advance you on your way more than great efforts in which you would break down.

Harriet Monsell by T. T. Carter, p. 157. A letter.

W. H. LONGRIDGE

Great opportunities of suffering for Christ may not be for such as I am. But there are many little opportunities which can be used by every generous soul; little acts of mortification; the sacrifice of one's own will, tastes, and natural inclinations; not complaining when I have good reason to do so; putting up with the faults of those I have to live with.

It is by using occasions such as these that I shall grow in devotion to Jesus crucified. "If you have a real desire to find and possess Jesus" says St John of the Cross, "do not attempt to seek Him without the cross."

Retreats for Priests, p. 244.

ROBERT NELSON

Conform your self to the will of God in those afflictions which he sends you. It is agreed, that 'tis our duty to submit to what God in his wisdom shall lay upon us; and that we should always pray, that *his will may be done*. However, it is very necessary that I should warn you against an ill practice, too common among those that are otherways very devout: they are apt to declare their readiness to suffer, when the will of God makes it their duty, to which they desire to conform themselves; but they would fain excuse themselves from the present affliction that lies upon them, and think any other would be easy to them; but that which they endure, always appears to them unreasonable: they complain, it hinders their endeavours after Christian perfection; and that, instead of improving their virtue, it increases their guilt. The man who is touched in his reputation, declares how willingly he would submit to any other affliction that could befall him; but he is not able to bear such injurious reflections, they strike too near his heart. The sick man, that is confin'd to his bed, which is irksome and very tiresome, complains that his distemper makes him impatient and discontented, and prevents the practice of several good works he design'd, if free from his sickness. The woman, who meets with a perverse husband, and with obstinate, disobedient children, would suffer willingly any other affliction, except that which lies upon her, which she imagines can only serve to increase her misery in this life and the next. In short, there is almost nobody but who would be willing to exchange their present cross for another, and think themselves unhappy in the particular sort of their sufferings; whence it proceeds, that their minds are always unquiet, and that they never perfectly resign themselves to the will of God.

Now all this management is very unreasonable, for is it not God that sends or permits that particular affliction? Does not the manner of your suffering come from his hand? Is it for you to determine what He ought to do? And ought you to prescribe to Him the particular cross He should lay upon you? Banish all such thoughts from your mind, and let the cross which He sends you be received with resignation and satisfaction, though it may be it is not what you would have chose for your self: it is sufficient to make you contented and quiet, that it comes from God; and that therefore it is by this affliction that He designs to make your calling and election sure.

The Practice of True Devotion, ch. 7, sec. 8.

JOHN TAULER

To this I reply that external practices are good and useful if they are used in an orderly manner and in moderation; and if, over and above them, a man examines and watches himself internally, and giveth himself up to God.

The Following of Christ, English ed. by J. K. Morell, p. 31.

WALTER HILTON

For wit thou well that what man or woman shall be occupied ghostly in thoughts, reasonable pain of hunger wilfully taken, of sickness in the stomach or in the head or in other part of the body, for default of himself by too mickle fasting or in any other wise, shall mickle let the spirit and mickle hinder him from the knowing and the beholding of ghostly things, unless he have the more grace. For though it be so that bodily pain, either of penance or of sickness, or else bodily occupation, sometimes letteth not the fervour of love to God in devotion, but often increaseth it; soothly I expect that it letteth the fervour of love in contemplation, which may not be had nor felt soberly, but in great rest of body and of soul. For this do thou reasonably that longeth to thee, and keep thy bodily kind upon reason, and suffer God then send what that He will, be it health or sickness. Take it gladly, and grouch not against God wilfully.

The Scale of Perfection, p. 186.

LORENZO SCUPOLI

This has been the end of many, who, following presumptuously the impulse of an indiscreet zeal, have, in their excessive outward austerities, gone beyond the measure of their own virtue, and so have perished in their own inventions, and become the sport of malicious fiends. This would not have befallen them, had they well considered what we have been saying, and remembered that these acts of painful self-discipline, though praiseworthy and profitable in those who have corresponding strength of body and humility of spirit, must yet be attempered to each man's state and condition.

The Spiritual Combat, ch. 42.

Yet must thou not indiscreetly impose penances upon thyself, nor seek opportunities of suffering for the love of God, under the sole guidance of thine own will; but with the advice of thy spiritual father, and of thy superiors, who will rule thee in the place of God; Who through their means, disposes thy will, and does with it what He wills, and as He wills. Yet thou shalt not do what thou wouldest; but let God do in thee what He wills.

The Path to Paradise, ch. 5.

GABRIELLE BOSSIS

[Christ speaking to the soul]

Give me little things.

(While I was thinking: "If I left all these theatre tours so as to free myself for solitude.") Peter fleeing from Rome met me on the road: "Master, where are you going?" "Peter, I am going to Rome to be crucified in your place."

Do not think that a saint necessarily appears a saint in the eyes of men. For he has his exterior nature. It is the interior which counts. Some fruits which have a wrinkled, or even prickly skin, give no hint of the sweet and juicy taste inside. It is the same with My saints: their value is in their heart.

Remember: all that causes pride perishes and turns to shame.

All that makes for humility bears fruit and turns to its glory.

LUI et moi. Entretiens spirituels, vol. vii. (7 volumes. Beauchesne, Paris.)

FRANÇOIS FÉNELON

You ought to reserve hours for reading, prayer and resting your mind and body in the presence of God.

Do not anticipate crosses. You would perhaps seek some which God would not want to give you, and which would be incompatible with his plans for you. But embrace unhesitatingly all those which his hand offers you every moment. There is a providence for crosses, as for the necessities of life. It is the daily bread which feeds the soul, and which God never fails to distribute to us. If you were in a more free state, more serene, more unhampered, you would have more to fear in too soft a life. But yours will always have its bitterness, while you are faithful.

I beg you, urgently, to stay in peace in this right and simple conduct. In depriving yourself of this liberty by straining after far-fetched mortifications, you would lose those which God is jealous of preparing for you himself, and you would harm yourself under the pretext of advancing. Be free, gay, simple, a child.

Christian Perfection, tr. by Mildred Whitney Stillman, p. 21.

FRANÇOIS GUILLORÉ

We are all ready to talk about self-sacrifice and voluntary mortification. But instead of dwelling upon fancied sacrifices, accept those which come upon you through distraction in prayer, the loss of sensible enjoyment in it which other men have, the humiliation of becoming conscious of having but a weak wandering imagination—and you will win some precious lessons.

Self-Renunciation, p. 78.

But, nevertheless, bear in mind that it is not right to overwhelm your body, and that all such practices should be proportioned to its strength, otherwise your penitence degenerates into indiscretion. God does not lead all men by these paths, and self-will may destroy any good you might gain from them. Therefore all such discipline should be used under direction, and both to guard against your mistakes, and because all conquest of the body is with an ulterior aim to that of the spirit, submission to guidance is a valuable assistance.

Ibid., p. 293f.

PHILIP DODDRIDGE

May mine eyes be watchful to observe the descent of mercies from thee; and may a grateful sense of thine hand add a relish to all! and when afflictions come, which, in a world like this, I would accustom myself to expect, may I remember that they come from thee; and may that fully reconcile me to them; while I firmly believe, that the same love which gives us our daily bread, appoints us our daily crosses; which I would learn to take up, that I may follow my dear Lord, with a temper like that which he manifested, when ascending Calvary for my sake; saying like him, "The cup which my Father hath given me, shall I not drink it?"

The Rise and Progress of Religion in the Soul, ch. 19.

WILLIAM ROMAINE

He tries thee with one cross, and thou art dissatisfied, thou couldst contrive a better for thyself. Thou wouldst be thine own lord and governor. Self-will, they say, is a sure guide to self-destruction. Beware then of thine own will. When God calls thee to take up any cross, don't wish for another. He sends this, and to it he requires thy submission.

Walk of Faith, ch. 9.

DISTRACTION AND DRYNESS

W. H. LONGRIDGE

We are not to think that our meditation has been badly made because we have had few or no lights or consolations, or because we have been much tried with wandering thoughts, aridity, or even diabolical temptations. If, in spite of these obstacles, we have really tried our best to preserve the full time in prayer, and to reject wandering thoughts and temptations, however violent and insistent, to be patient in dryness, and to keep ourselves as best we can in the presence of God, then we may be sure our meditation has not been unfruitful. We may not feel it at the time, but God, we may be sure, has been secretly pouring His grace into our hearts, and we shall find afterwards that we have received blessing and strength.

The Spiritual Exercises of St Ignatius of Loyola, p. 72.

St Ignatius would have us earnestly protest before God that we come to our meditation, not to receive consolation or for any motive of self-interest, but purely for the service and praise of His divine Majesty. To enter upon prayer in this spirit of detachment and self-surrender is one of the great secrets of making it well, as also of persevering in times of dryness and desolation.

Ibid., p. 53.

ST TERESA OF AVILA

You may think that you will be full of determination to resist outward trials if God will only grant you inward favours. His Majesty knows best what is suitable for us; it is not for us to advise Him what to give us, for He can rightly reply that we know not what we ask. All that the beginner in prayer has to do— and you must not forget this, for it is very important—is to labour and be resolute and prepare himself with all possible diligence to bring his will into conformity with the will of God.

Interior Castle, 2nd Mansions, ch. 1. *Complete Works*, p. 216.

. . . so that these periods of aridity may teach you to be humble, and not make you restless, which is the aim of the devil. Be sure that, where there is true humility, even if God never grants the soul favours, He will give it peace and resignation to His will, with which it may be more content than others are with favours.

Interior Castle, 3rd Mansions, ch. 1. *Complete Works*, p. 223.

JULIAN OF NORWICH

Therefore he saith thus: Pray inwardly, though thee thinketh it savour thee not: for it is profitable, though thou feel not, though thou see nought; yea, though thou think thou canst not. For in dryness and barrenness, in sickness and in feebleness, then is thy prayer well-pleasant to me, though thee thinketh it savour thee nought but little. And so is all thy believing prayer in my sight.

Revelations of Divine Love, p. 85.

And yet nevertheless when this sweetness is hid, we fall again into blindness, and so into woe and tribulation in diverse manners. But then is this our comfort, that *we know in our faith* that by virtue of Christ which is our Keeper, we assent never thereto, but we groan there-against, and dare on, in pain and woe, praying, unto that time that He sheweth Him again to us.

Ibid., p. 123.

And this word: *Thou shalt not be overcome*, was said full clearly and full mightily, for assuredness and comfort against all tribulations that may come. He said not: *Thou shalt not be tempested, thou shalt not be travailed, thou shalt not be afflicted*; but He said: *Thou shalt not be overcome.*

Ibid., p. 170.

LORENZO SCUPOLI

Many are the blessings which spiritual bitterness and dryness brings to the soul, if only it be received with all humility and patience. Did man but understand this, he would doubtless feel less disquiet and grief when overtaken by it; because he would look upon it not as a sign of his Lord's hatred, but of His great and special love; and he would receive it as a signal favour vouchsafed to him.

Of inward peace or *The Path to Paradise*, p. 227.

Hence he, who once thought himself to be something comes, by the use of this bitter medicine, sent him from heaven, to count himself the vilest of men, and even unworthy of the name of Christian: nor would he ever have come to such a low estimation of himself, nor to such deep humility, had not great tribulations and these strange temptations forced him to it. For one favour which God confers in this life upon the soul that has wholly placed and resigned herself into His Hands, is to medicine her as He pleases, and with such medicines as He alone perfectly knows to be necessary to her health and well-being.

Ibid., p. 230.

THOMAS MERTON

And so although this sense of peace may be a sign that we are united to God it is still only a sign—an accident. The substance of the union may be had without any such sense, and sometimes when we have no feeling of peace or of God's presence He is more truly present to us than He has ever been before.

Seeds of Contemplation, p. 77.

Prayer and love are learned in the hour when prayer has become impossible and your heart has turned to stone.

Ibid., p. 82.

JUAN DE AVILA

And persevere in this, [reading and prayer] however great the aridity, offering to the Lord this time which thou hast spent. He will accept it, for from Him came the command to spend it thus.

Quoted in *Studies of the Spanish Mystics*, tr. by E. Alison Peers, 1st ed., vol. ii, p. 133. (Rev. ed., vol. ii, p. 104.)

ST PETER OF ALCANTARA

Firstly, for those who lack spiritual consolation the remedy is as follows: do not, on this account, abandon the customary exercise of prayer, though it appear insipid to you, and of little fruit, but rather prostrate yourself in the presence of God as a guilty sinner . . . and experience, at least, shows that every time a man perseveres in prayer, with a little attention and care in doing his best honestly, he comes forth consoled and joyful at seeing that, on his part, he has done something of what in him lay.

Treatise on Prayer and Meditation, pp. 131f.

JEAN PIERRE CAMUS

Blessed indeed is the soul which continues stedfast amid all that dryness and sensible desolation which is the crucible wherein the pure gold of love is refined and purified. Blessed is he who bears the proving trial patiently; "After He hath proved me, I shall come forth as gold."

The Spirit of St Francis de Sales, p. 20.

FRANÇOIS GUILLORÉ

If God pleases to take all power of delight in prayer from you, offer to Him a submissive will, and be thankful that you have somewhat to offer.

Self-Renunciation, p. 75.

CHARLES DE CONDREN

For the third point concerning your prayer, the light of God sometimes shines there in the shadows; there is a great difference between the light of God which is invisible and incomprehensible to us, and which, being divine, is apt to satisfy God and not to satisfy our own senses or spirit, and the light of our own spirit which is more sensible and satisfying to us, and which sustains our self-satisfaction, and estranges us from the true light of God.

Lettres, p. 397.

PHILIP DODDRIDGE

But while the darkness continues, "go on in the way of your duty". Continue the use of means and ordinances: read and meditate: pray, yes and sing the praises of God too; though it may be with a heavy heart. Follow the footsteps of his flock; you may perhaps meet the Shepherd of souls in doing it.

The Rise and Progress of Religion in the Soul, ch. 23.

WILLIAM ROMAINE

Thy God has most gracious designs towards thee in putting thee into the fire. It is to try thy faith; whether thou canst trust him there. It is to improve thy faith by the trial, that thou mayest trust him more. If thou hast trusting faith, it is to teach thee patient faith. It is a hard lesson to learn to trust against sense and carnal reason, and to say, This cross is good for me, I desire to submit, and to take it patiently at the hand of God.

Walk of Faith, ch. 9.

THE WHOLE DUTY OF MAN

This wandering in Prayer is a thing we are much concerned to arm ourselves against, it being that to which we are naturally wonderfully prone. . . . And if thou dost thus sincerely and diligently strive against them, either God will enable thee in some measure to overcome them, or he will in his mercy pardon thee what thou canst not prevent.

Sunday V.

DETACHMENT OR INDIFFERENCE

W. H. LONGRIDGE

We come lastly to the second practical conclusion, which contains within itself the germ of all that spiritual perfection to which the Exercises are designed to lead us on. If we are to be guided by the above rule, using or abstaining from creatures according as, and just as far as, they help or hinder us in the pursuit of our end, it is "necessary that we should make ourselves indifferent to all created things, in all that is left to the liberty of our free-will, and is not forbidden; in such sort that we do not for our part wish for health more than sickness, for wealth more than poverty, for honour more than dishonour, for a long life more than a short one, and so in all other things; desiring and choosing only that which leads us more directly to the end for which we were created."

The Spiritual Exercises of St Ignatius of Loyola, p. 42.

JOHN CHAPMAN

The Virtue of Poverty means complete detachment: we are not to depend on things, but they on us. (1) This is a thing we can practise, as beginners; (2) a little further on towards perfection it is more like a gift, not to be obtained by practice or activity on our part, but merely by loving God more. So you will get detachment from *things* and from *self*, by merely giving yourself to God, and *accepting yourself* as you find yourself to be. We all have one unpleasant person to live with, whom we can't get away from —ourself. Put up with yourself, and take your own hated imperfection and weakness as an unpleasantness you have to bear with. It is very hard, but it is really a very perfect act of love to God.

Spiritual Letters, 62, p. 156.

ST FRANCIS DE SALES

Love nought overmuch, I implore you, not even those graces which one sometimes loses by exaggerating them. . . . What I wish is that you should not torment yourselves by desires or in any way (such as by too much chagrin at your faults), which ceases to be pure when it disquiets you.

Œuvres, xiii, 53, 305, 167.

ST JOHN OF THE CROSS

Wherefore the eyes of the soul must ever be withdrawn from all these apprehensions which it can see and understand distinctly, which are communicated through sense, and do not produce the sure foundation of faith, and must be set upon that which it sees not, and which belongs not to sense, but to spirit, which can be expressed by no figures of sense; and it is this which leads the soul to union in faith, which is the true medium, as has been said.

Ascent of Mount Carmel, bk ii, *Complete Works*, p. 136.

The feelings can only serve as motives for love if the will desires to pass beyond them, and not otherwise; and thus delectable feelings do not of themselves lead the soul to God, but cause it to rest in themselves; but in the operation of the will, which is to love God, the soul sets on Him alone its affection, joy, pleasure, contentment and love, leaving all things behind and loving Him above them all.

Letter XI, ibid., bk iii, p. 280.

ST TERESA OF AVILA

Perhaps we do not know what love is: it would not surprise me a great deal to learn this, for love consists, not in the extent of our happiness, but in the firmness of our determination to try to please God in everything, and to endeavour, in all possible ways, not to offend Him, and to pray Him ever to advance the honour and glory of His Son and the growth of the Catholic Church. Those are the signs of love; do not imagine that the important thing is never to be thinking of anything else and that if your mind becomes slightly distracted all is lost.

Interior Castle, 4th Mansions, ch. 1. *Complete Works*, p. 233.

MARTIN LUTHER

The impure and perverted lovers [of God] who are nothing else than parasites and seek their own advantage in God, neither love nor praise His bare goodness, but have an eye to themselves and consider only how God is good to them, that is, how deeply He makes them feel His goodness and how many good things He does to them. They esteem Him highly, are filled with joy and sing His praises, so long as this feeling continues, but as soon as ever He hides His face and withdraws the rays of His goodness, leaving them bare and in misery, their love and praise are at an end. They delight in their salvation much more than in their Saviour, in the gift more than in the Giver.

Works, VII, 556, Quoted in *The Catholicity of Protestantism*, pp. 72f.

WALTER HILTON

For in virtues and in knowing of God with love is no deceit. But all such manner of feelings may be good, wrought by a good angel, and they may be deceivable, feigned by a wicked angel, when he transfigureth him into an angel of light.

Scale of Perfection, p. 19.

THOMAS MERTON

It is not enough to possess and enjoy material and spiritual things within the limits of rational moderation: we must be able to rise above all joy and pass beyond all possession if we will come to the pure possession and enjoyment of God.

Seeds of Contemplation, p. 76.

ST PETER OF ALCANTARA

We should note that this intercourse with God being, as the Wise Man says, something very delightful and agreeable, it comes about that many persons, gripped by this sweetness, which surpasses all power of description attach themselves to God and devote themselves to every kind of spiritual exercise, reading, prayer, the frequentation of the sacraments, precisely on account of the great relish they experience therein, in such sort that the main object they have in view, and the one which leads them forward, is this wonderful sweetness for which they long. Here, indeed, is a great and very widespread error into which many fall. The principle end of all our works should be to love God and to seek after God, whereas these are much rather loving themselves and seeking after themselves. One's own personal relish and contentment, that is the end philosophers propose to themselves in their speculations. "This", says a learned writer, "is a species of avarice, of luxury and spiritual greed, and it is no less perilous than that which is sensual."

What is even worse than that, from this error another, no less evil, arises, which is to judge oneself and others according to these feelings of devotional relish, fancying that each one has more or less perfection according as he enjoys in a greater or less degree this relish of God. This is a complete mistake.

Against these two errors, here is a piece of advice of general application: let each one grasp once for all that the end of all these exercises and of the whole spiritual life is simply obedience to the commandments of God and the accomplishment of the divine will. To achieve this we must die to our own will, that thus the will of God, which is in opposition to it, may live and reign.

Treatise on Prayer and Meditation, pt 2, pp. 142f.

ESSENCE OF PRAYER

ST IGNATIUS OF LOYOLA

Annotation III. As in all the spiritual Exercises that follow we make use of the understanding when reasoning, and of the will when exciting affections, let us take notice that in acts of the will, when we are conversing vocally or mentally with God our Lord or with His Saints, greater reverence is required on our part than when we make use of the understanding in Reasoning.

[On which Fr W. H. Longridge, comments:]

In the use of the understanding, we converse as it were with ourselves; in the acts of the will, we address ourselves to God. The work of the understanding is chiefly a preparation for prayer; but the acts of the will are prayer itself.

The Spiritual Exercises of St Ignatius of Loyola, p. 9.

JOHN CHAPMAN

It is right, I think, to feel perfectly satisfied (after our prayer) that it *is* all right when it *feels* all wrong. We humble ourselves and say: "O God, I cannot pray. I cannot even keep in thy presence." Or, "I cannot pray as I did yesterday; but I only want to do Thy will, not to be satisfied with my prayer."

It is of the very essence of prayer that it does not depend upon us. It depends on circumstances—our stomach, our preoccupations, much more than on our will—for the character it takes; and, naturally, on God's special grace. But possibly the *best* kind is when we seem unable to do anything, if then we throw ourselves on God, and stay contentedly before Him; worried, anxious, tired, listless, but—above all and under it all—humbled and abandoned to His will, contented with our own discontent.

Spiritual Letters, 51, p. 132.

JEREMY TAYLOR

And yet prayer, that does all this, is of itself nothing but an ascent of the mind to God, a desiring things fit to be desired, and an expression of this desire to God as we can, and as becomes us. And our unwillingness to pray is nothing else but a not desiring what we ought passionately to long for; or if we do desire it, it is a choosing rather to miss our satisfaction and felicity than to ask for it.

Holy Living, ch. 4, sec. 7.

ST JEANNE DE CHANTAL

The great method of prayer is to have none. If in going to prayer one can form in oneself a pure capacity for receiving the spirit of God, that will suffice for all method. Prayer should be accomplished by grace and not by artifice.

Quoted by Henri Bremond, *A Literary History of Religious Thought in France*, vol. ii, p. 423.

PIERRE DE BÉRULLE

Persevere in the application of your soul to the Divine Essence and to the Holy Trinity, and this do rather by reverence than by intellect, by simplicity rather than by art and subtlety. For this untreated Object is so far above all created things, that we must rather lose and sink ourselves in Him than seek to know Him, and we belong to Him through His own hidden operations rather than by our own thoughts and conceptions. Desire to be and to belong to this Divine Essence, so intimate, so present, so mighty in working by ways in which it may please Him to appoint for your soul, without your knowledge or pleasure, or the limiting of you to all that you might imagine or form in yourself.

Œuvres, pp. 138f. Quoted by Bremond, ibid., vol. iii, p. 110.

JOHN TAULER

Love is twofold, one springeth from the understanding, and with this *will* one cannot love Him in His eternity; the other ariseth from faith, and loveth Him for the sake of His eternity. As we can and must believe that God is without beginning and without end, so also can the will love Him entirely from the light of faith, as an always existing and everlasting God.

The Following of Christ, vol. ii, p. 81.

JULIAN OF NORWICH

The seeking, with faith, hope, and charity, pleaseth our Lord, and the finding pleaseth the soul and fulfilleth it with joy. And thus was I learned, to mine understanding, that seeking is as good as beholding, for the time that He will suffer the soul to be in travail. It is God's will that *we seek Him*, to the beholding of Him, for by *that* He shall shew us Himself of His special grace when He will.

Revelations of Divine Love, p. 24.

The saints that be in Heaven, they will to know nothing but that which our Lord willeth to shew them: and also their charity and their desire is ruled after the will of our Lord: and thus we ought to will like to them. Then shall we nothing will nor desire but the will of our Lord, as they do: for we are all one in God's seeing.

Ibid., p. 62.

THOMAS TRAHERNE

He willed the redemption of mankind, and therefore is His Son Jesus Christ an infinite treasure. Unless you will it too, He will be no treasure to you. Verily you ought to will these things so ardently that God himself should be therefore your joy because He willed them. Your will ought to be united to Him in all places of His dominion. Were you not born to have communion with Him? And that cannot be without this heavenly union. Which when it is what it ought is Divine and Infinite.

Centuries of Meditation, p. 53.

EVAGRIUS PONTICUS

Do not pray that things may be according to your desires, for they are not always in keeping with the will of God. Better pray as you were taught saying: "Thy will be done" on me (Matt. vi. 10). And ask thus about all things, for He always desires what is good and profitable for your soul, whereas you do not always seek it.

Attr. St Nilus of Sinai, *Early Fathers from the Philokalia*, p. 131f.

THOMAS MERTON

But in all these things, it is the will to pray that is the essence of prayer, and the desire to find God and to see Him and to love Him is the one thing that matters. If you have desired to know Him and love Him you have already done what was expected of you, and it is much better to desire God without being able to think clearly of Him, than to have marvellous thoughts about Him without desiring to enter into union with His will.

Seeds of Contemplation, p. 84.

AUGUSTINE MORRIS

There are indeed only two rules of prayer: Pray as the Holy Spirit would have you pray, which is another way of saying, Pray as you best can pray; and the other is, Go on praying. Not that our prayers should necessarily be long: even monks are not expected to remain for hours in a state of prayer, for St Benedict counsels them that prayer should be short and pure. But perseverence in prayer day by day through life is what we here commend: Go on praying, somehow or other, however best you can manage it, go on praying. The very fact that you are kneeling at your bedside or adopting any other posture of prayer is in itself an *act* of adoration, and worth something at least, though your mind be elsewhere. Be gentle with yourself, however. Try quietly to concentrate your thoughts again, and do not be discouraged if they wander again and yet again. Do not give way because your heart is cold, and prayer seems useless. Provided you persevere, the trouble will pass. In the meantime, distracted and cold though your prayer may be, you are possibly offering more to God than you did when prayer was a joy; for now you are offering something at some cost to yourself. At all costs, therefore, go on praying; and you will then be among that glorious band of true worshippers whom the Father seeketh to worship Him. You will be doing now in pain upon earth what it will be your indescribable bliss to do in everlasting joy in heaven.

Straight Course to God, pp. 68f.

DIEGO DE ESTELLA

Contemplation is the work of the understanding, and the road and means to perfection; but perfection consists in the raising of our will to God by Divine union and sovereign love.

[Note: The word "contemplation" here is used in a different sense from its usual use.]

Quoted in *Studies of the Spanish Mystics*, 1st ed., vol. ii, p. 236. (Rev. ed., vol. ii, p. 185.)

ST PETER OF ALCANTARA

Let each one grasp once for all that the end of all these exercises and of the whole spiritual life is simply obedience to the commandments of God and the accomplishment of the divine will. To achieve this we must die to our own will, that thus the will of God, which is in opposition to it, may live and reign.

Treatise on Prayer and Meditation, pt 2, p. 143.

PHILIP DODDRIDGE

Therefore you can hardly be too frequently told, that religion consists chiefly, *"in the resolution of the will for God, and in a constant care to avoid whatever we are persuaded he would disapprove, to dispatch the work he has assigned us in life, and to promote his glory in the happiness of mankind"*.

The Rise and Progress of Religion in the Soul, ch. 21.

WILLIAM ROMAINE

Through mine ignorance and selfwill I thought thy cross was a punishment, and I used wickedly to despise the chastening of the Lord. Pardon thy servant concerning this thing. Forgive mine opposition to thy cross, and subdue mine impatient desire to shake it off. Holy Father, mortify my will, and make it bow to thine. Thy will be done in me, and by me. . . . Thine be the praise for shewing me the need of suffering, and of renewing me by it in the inward man to a conformity to thy holy will. I now see thy love herein.

Walk of Faith, ch. 9.

VITALIS LEHODEY

In our opinion, the whole essence of active contemplation is contained in these two words: *it looks and it loves*.

The Ways of Mental Prayer, p. 192.

JUAN FALCONI

The Saints . . . teach that all the faithful must ever believe that God is present and that they must walk in His presence; the which is naught else than to be gazing at God with a simple regard; and this is contemplation.

Quoted in *Studies of the Spanish Mystics*, 1st ed., vol. ii, p. 372. (Rev. ed., vol. ii, p. 292.)

ST FRANCIS DE SALES

In conclusion, Meditation is the mother, and Contemplation the daughter of love, and for this reason I called Contemplation a loving attention, for children are named after their fathers, and not fathers after their children.

Treatise on the Love of God, bk vi, p. 241.

WILLIAM WILBERFORCE

But the passion, which alone the Holy Scriptures dignify with the name of Love, is a deep, not a superficial feeling; a fixed and permanent, not an occasional emotion. It proves the validity of its title by actions corresponding with its nature, by practical endeavours to gratify the wishes, and to promote the interests, of the object of affection: "If a man love me, he will keep my sayings." "This is the love of God, that we keep his commandments." This, therefore, is the best standard by which to try the quality, or, the quality being ascertained, to estimate the strength, of the religious affections. Without suffering ourselves to derive too much complacency from transient fervours of devotion, we should carefully and frequently prove ourselves by this less doubtful test; impartially examining our daily conduct; and often comparing our actual with our possible services; the fair amount of our exertions, with our natural or acquired means and opportunities of usefulness.

A Practical View of the Prevailing Religious System of Professed Christians, ch. 3, sec. 2.

GUIDANCE

ST FRANCIS DE SALES

And even in matters of moment we are to use a great humility, and not to think that we can find out God's will by force of examination and subtlety of discourse; but having implored the light of the Holy Ghost, applied our consideration to the seeking of his good-pleasure, taken the counsel of our director, and, perhaps, of two or three other spiritual persons, we must resolve and determine in the name of God, and must not afterwards question our choice, but devoutly, peacefully, and firmly keep and pursue it.

Treatise on the Love of God, bk viii, p. 363.

KENNETH E. KIRK

Cassian (Collat. ii.14.15) makes the interesting observation that the Holy Spirit is not wont to reveal directly to men anything that may be learnt through human teachers. Thus Samuel, though directly called by the Holy Spirit, must go to Eli for an interpretation of the voice. Saul, on the Damascus road, is converted by the vision of our Lord, 'yet Almighty God, notwithstanding that He sees him so well disposed, does not disclose his designs. And why? Because there is in Damascus a priest, Ananias by name to whom he can make application. "Go to him", says our Lord, "and learn from him what I will have you to do."'

Some Principles of Moral Theology, p. 134n.

JEREMY TAYLOR

Since God will be justified with a free obedience, and there is an obedience of understanding as well as of will and affection, it is of great concernment, as to be willing to believe whatever God says, so also to enquire diligently whether the Will of God be so as is pretended. Even our acts of understanding are acts of choice; and therefore it is commanded as a duty to "search the scriptures", to "try the spirits whether they be of God or no", "of ourselves to be able to judge what is right", to "try all things" and to "retain what is best". For he that resolves not to consider, resolves not to be careful whether he have the truth or no.

Liberty of Prophesying. Quoted by Margaret Cropper, *Flame touches Flame*, p. 114.

JEREMY DREXELIUS

Seventh Rule. No one discovers the Divine Will with greater certainty than he who with perfect sincerity desires to conform himself to it in all things. This desire is, in truth, the thread for unravelling the mazes of all labyrinths. All uncertainty about the Divine Will is removed, if, when one is ignorant as to what God wills, or which of two lawful things He would rather have done, he is yet so disposed in mind as to say with perfect sincerity of intention—"If I knew, O Lord, what Thou willest to be done by me in this matter, I would immediately do it." When this protestation has been made, let him unhesitatingly do what he will, and cease to disturb himself, for he will not easily offend against the Divine Will. . . . We best learn to *know* the Will of God *by doing it.*

The Heliotropium, bk i, pp. 36f.

PENITENCE

AUGUSTINE BAKER

Yea, souls that are of such a disposition [those who are given to scruples or disquiet or dejection] ought, even in the beginning, after their first conversion, not to dwell upon the exercises that concern remorse for sin or other matters of fear, as death, judgment, and hell, but rather to fix upon affections contrary to their present disposition; and in case of new faults committed, let their contrition or detestation of sin be rather exercised in a generality, or virtually in acts of conversion to God, than particularly, directly, and expressly; and let them not be scrupulous herein, out of an opinion that at such times God expects painful remorses from them, or earnest expressions of detestation of their sins; for such detestation is sufficiently involved in an act of direct love to God, which contains much perfection besides. Such acts, therefore, being more beneficial to her, are consequently more acceptable to God.

Holy Wisdom, sec. 3, p. 10.

ST TERESA OF AVILA

We get a distorted idea of our own nature, and, if we never stop thinking about ourselves, I am not surprised if we experience these fears and others which are still worse. It is for this reason, daughters, that I say we must set our eyes upon Christ our God, from Whom we shall learn true humility, and also upon His saints.

Interior Castle, 1st Mansion, ch. 2. *Complete works*, p. 209.

JEAN-JACQUES OLIER

Therefore I counsel you not to reflect so much upon yourself. For although this may be under the pretext of self-purification and sanctification, it is nevertheless . . . (although this may be unknown to you, some) *self-satisfaction in you*. We must be wholly all in our All, Who is the Source of all holiness and light.

Lettres, I, 296f. Quoted by Bremond, op. cit., vol. iii, p. 410.

CHARLES DE CONDREN

Eschew as though it were a hell the consideration of yourself and your offences. No one should ever think of these things except to humiliate himself and love our Lord. It is enough to regard yourself *in general* as a sinner, even as there are many saints in heaven who were such.

Quoted by Aldous Huxley, *The Perennial Philosophy*, pp. 262f.

JULIAN OF NORWICH

For he saith: "Accuse not thyself overmuch, deeming that thy tribulation and thy woe is all for thy fault; for I will not that thou be heavy or sorrowful indiscreetly. For I tell thee, howsoever thou do, thou shalt have woe. And therefore I will that thou wisely know thy penance; and thou shalt see in truth that all thy living is penance profitable.

Revelations of Divine Love, p. 188.

LORENZO SCUPOLI

If, then, when thou fallest, thou art so saddened and disquieted, as to be tempted to despair of advancing and doing well, this is a sure sign that thou trustest in thyself and not in God.

And this sadness and despondency will be the greater, by how much thou hast trusted to thyself and distrusted God. For he who has any large measure of mistrust of self and trust in God, feels neither surprise, nor despondency, nor bitterness, when he falls, knowing that this has been brought upon him by his own weakness and want of trust in God. On the contrary, more mistrustful of self, more humbly trustful in God, he pursues his enterprise, and follows after his enemies to the death, with a spirit more undaunted and resolute than before; hating, above all things, his fault, and the unruly passions which have occasioned his fall; and mourning, with a deep and quiet and patient sorrow, over his offence against God.

The Spiritual Combat, ch. 4.

There are also many persons who deceive themselves in this manner. They mistake the uneasiness and fear consequent upon sin for virtuous emotions; and know not that these feelings, painful as they are, spring from wounded pride and presumption, founded on confidence in self. Thinking themselves to be something, they have unduly relied upon their own strength. Their fall proves to them the vanity of such reliance, and then they are troubled and astonished as at some strange thing, and are disheartened to see the support on which they had rashly placed their confidence, sink to the ground.

This never happens to the humble man, who confiding in his God alone, presumes in nothing upon himself. Though grieved when he falls into any fault, he is neither surprised nor disquieted for he knows that his own misery and weakness, already clearly manifest to himself by the light of truth, have brought all this upon him.

Ibid., ch. 5.

ST MARK THE ASCETIC

If you wish to bring a blameless confession to God, do not recollect your past faults in appearance (in detail), but suffer their results with courage.

A man of experience who has learnt the truth, confesses to God not by recollection of what he has done, but by enduring what befalls him.

153 and 155 of 226 Texts, *Early Fathers from the Philokalia*, p. 91.

AUGUSTINE MORRIS

Ultimately, we can only come to humility by looking outside and above ourselves, that is, to God. The more we look at God the more we shall grow like him, and humility will grow in our souls unperceived by ourselves, like the automatic growth of the seed of which our Lord speaks in the little parable which is the only one recorded by St Mark alone. "So is the kingdom of God, as if a man should cast seed in the earth; and should sleep and rise night and day, and the seed should spring up and grow, he knoweth not how." (Mark 4.26,27.) The truest humility is not self-depreciation, but self-forgetfulness. But to this we may only come by constant waiting upon God and service of our fellow-men for his sake.

Straight Course to God, p. 45.

GABRIELLE BOSSIS

[Christ speaking to the soul]

Offer yourself to Me just as you are. Do not wait to be satisfied with yourself. Unite yourself to Me in your greatest wretchedness [misères]. I take you, I redeem you, if you give Me your trust. Have trust. Who loves you better?

LUI et moi. Entretiens spirituels, vol. viii, p. 174. (7 volumes. Beauchesne, Paris.)

As I recalled to Him my sins. "Why are you astonished that you have faults? Are you not one of the most miserable? Is it not to wretchedness [misères] that I love to give Myself?"

Ibid., p. 213.

JEAN PIERRE CAMUS

In like manner he could not endure sadness and anxiety, believing with St Thomas that peace and joy are the greatest signs of love. Thus to one who was yielding to depression he writes:—"Be at peace, and let your soul feed upon the sweetness of heavenly love, without which our hearts were lifeless, our life joyless. What should sadden one who serves our Everlasting Joy? Nothing save sin ought to vex or grieve us; and even when sorry for sin, holy joy and hope should come to the rescue."

The Spirit of St Francis de Sales, p. 275.

FRANÇOIS FÉNELON

When an involuntary memory comes of past wretchedness, we have only to remain overcome and annihilated before God, carrying peacefully before his adorable face all the shame and all the ignominy of our sins without nevertheless seeking to dwell on or to recall this memory.

Christian Perfection, p. 25.

NO VIOLENCE

ST FRANCIS DE SALES

We must do all by love and nothing by force: it is better to love obedience than to fear disobedience.

Œuvres, xii, 363.

CHARLES DE CONDREN

Do nothing by forcing your intellect or your spirit, but with true faith that you can, with Jesus Christ, by the virtue of His Spirit, do all that is useful to God's glory and the good of your soul.

Flee all disquietude of spirit, and all constraint in spiritual things. . . . Oh, how great a secret is it in the spiritual life to belong to God without attachment to anything else and *without choice of any means by which to honour Him* but with a perfect will to use for His Glory whatsoever His Providence may cause us to meet with, and to be one with Him in His Will thus.

Quoted by Bremond, op. cit., vol. iii, p. 339.

When there seems to be no opening for any new undertaking which one desires, one should remain quietly where one is, seeking to glorify God to the utmost in the position He assigns one for the time being, until it shall please Him to call one to some fresh work.

Quoted by H. L. S. Lear, *Priestly Life in France*, p. 26.

LORENZO SCUPOLI

That in order to fight successfully against his enemies, the soldier of Christ must avoid, as much as possible, all perturbations and disquiet of mind.

For on these accounts does our Lord God take pleasure in them; Whose Will bearing us on, we shall pass with a calm and quiet spirit through all the bitterness and contradictions of this life. And be sure that all disquiet on our part is displeasing in His sight; for of whatever nature it be, it is never free from imperfection, and always springs from some evil root of self-love.

The Spiritual Combat, ch. 25.

And if some movement of any sensual disquiet whatsoever arise within thy soul, be careful to calm it instantly, stilling thy heart, and suffering it not to wander or turn aside after any of these things. Do this whenever any thing occurs to disturb thee, whether in prayer, or at any other time; and know that thou wilt have learnt to pray aright when thou hast learnt thus to act; but observe, that all must be done with gentleness and without effort.

In short, the chief and constant exercise of thy life should be to quiet thy heart, and never suffer it to go astray.

The Path to Paradise, ch. 1.

ST ISAAC OF SYRIA

So long as a man makes efforts, striving to force the spiritual to come down to him, it resists. And if in his arrogance he dares to lift his eyes to the spiritual and strives to reach it by his understanding out of its proper time, his sight soon becomes dimmed.

Early Fathers from the Philokalia, p. 228.

FRANÇOIS FÉNELON

When we see during the prayer that our minds wander, we have only to bring them back quietly, without ever being discouraged by the annoyance of these so stubborn distractions. When they are involuntary, they can do no harm. On the contrary, they will help us more than a prayer accompanied by ardent feeling, because they humiliate us, mortify us and accustom us to seek God purely for himself, without the mingling of any pleasure.

Christian Perfection, p. 70.

FRANÇOIS GUILLORÉ

There are three things which are the groundwork of all perfection, and which are attainable by all who will seek them steadfastly. These are, first, a calm exterior; second, a quiet heart; and third, simplicity in our dealings with God.

Self-Renunciation, p. 8.

The third means whereby to attain a quiet heart is to leave the result of all you do to God. Yours be it to make use of whatever means are most suited to the desired object; but having done this, rest content, the issue and result is wholly and solely God's; leave Him to bring to pass whatever may be His Holy Will.

Ibid., p. 13.

E. M. GOULBURN

We have pointed out one method of obviating those distractions which are so baffling to Christian progress, and we will end by a general counsel to cultivate quietness of mind in all other ways as well as in this. Never shall we attain to holiness, so long as we are careful and troubled about many things. Cares and anxieties, even of a spiritual character, must be thrown upon God; the mind must be absolutely unburdened of them; and we must leave our Father to provide for them, when the need arises.

Thoughts on Personal Religion, p. 265.

ST TERESA OF AVILA

As I said first of all, I have already written to you about how you ought to behave when you have to suffer these disturbances with which the devil torments you; and about how recollection cannot be begun by making strenuous efforts, but must come gently, after which you will be able to practise it for longer periods at a time.

Interior Castle, 2nd Mansions. *Complete Works*, p. 218.

SUFFERING AND HARDSHIP

ST JOHN OF THE CROSS

There is another reason why the soul has walked securely in this darkness, and this is because it has been suffering; for the road of suffering is more secure and even more profitable than that of fruition and action: first, because in suffering the strength of God is added to that of man, while in action and fruition the soul is practising its own weakness and imperfections; and second, because in suffering the soul continues to practise and acquire the virtues and become purer, wiser and more cautious.

Dark Night of the Soul, bk ii, ch. 16. *Complete Works*, p. 452.

FRIEDRICH VON HÜGEL

She has caught the keynote to my thinking of all that is deepest in life and of all that is best in religion summed up in two inter-changeable terms (or rather terms which naturally complete each other) love and suffering.

Selected letters, p. 99.

For to suffer well is far more difficult than to act well (although the ordinary talk is that we just have to "grin and bear" suffering—we can do nothing to it or with it!!). Holy suffering is the very crown of holy action. And God is no pedant: He can and does look to the substance of our suffering, and knows how to penetrate beyond our surface restlessness or murmurs. Indeed, part of the great work suffering effects in the soul doubtless springs from the way in which, when acute, it almost invariably humbles us: we can much less easily cut a fine figure in our own eyes over our sufferings, than we can over our actions when in peace and plenty.

Selected Letters, p. 340.

KENNETH E. KIRK

It cannot be too clearly or too often emphasised that what is sometimes called "Christian resignation" is not in any sense whatever a Christian virtue. It is inspired indeed by a spirit the very reverse of Christian zeal. The true attitude of the converted Christian towards temptation is an active, not a passive resistance; towards suffering, trial and punishment, the resolve to endure not meekly but heroically. He goes to meet whatever befalls not as one making the best, as we say, of a bad business; but as one intending to prove himself more than a conqueror.

Some Principles of Moral Theology, p. 113.

CHARLES DE CONDREN

A common fault, but a very serious one among Christians, is that they reject the reality of that cross which they are so ready to adore in painting and sculpture. But if we only love the image, our love, be sure, is only imaginary too.

Quoted by Lear, op. cit., p. 204.

WILLIAM LAW

It is being made conformable to his Death, on which he founds his Hopes of sharing in the Resurrection of Christ. If Christians think that Salvation is now to be had on softer Terms, and that a Life of Indulgence and sensual Gratification is consistent with the Terms of the Gospel, and that they need not now be made conformable to his Death, they are miserably blind, and as such mistake their

Saviour, as the Worldly Jews who expected a temporal Messiah to deliver them.

Our Redemption is a Redemption by Sacrifice, and none are redeemed, but they who conform to it. *If we suffer with him we shall also reign with him.*

A Practical Treatise upon Christian Perfection, ch. 2.

SAMUEL RUTHERFORD

Stay and wait on till Christ loose the knot, that fasteneth his cross on your back; for he is coming to deliver: and I pray you, sister, learn to be worthy of his pains, who correcteth; and let him wring, and be ye washen; for he hath a Father's heart and a Father's hand, who is training you up, and making you meet for the high hall. This school of suffering is a preparation for the King's higher house; and let all your visitations speak all the letters of your Lord's summons.

Letter to Agnes Mackmath, 15 October 1640.

WORKS

ST FRANCIS DE SALES

Our works, therefore as a little grain of mustard-seed, are in no sort comparable in greatness to the tree of glory which they produce, yet they have the vigour and virtue to produce it, because they proceed from the Holy Spirit, who by an admirable infusion of his grace into our hearts makes our works his, and yet withal leaves them our own, since we are members of a head of which he is the Spirit, and ingrafted in a tree whereof he is the divine sap.

Treatise on the Love of God, bk xi, p. 481.

ST TERESA OF AVILA

This, my sisters, I should like us to strive to attain: we should desire and engage in prayer, not for our enjoyment, but for the sake of acquiring this strength which fits us for service.

Interior Castle, 7th Mansions, ch. 4. *Complete Works*, p. 348.

BENOIT DE CANFELD

Where many make a mistake is that, being commanded to do something, they murmur and excuse themselves, under pretext of being intent on what is spiritual, missing thus what they profess to seek, namely, God Who is all in work, and causing a threefold obstacle and darkness: first, the work itself; second, the fear of doing it; third, their own will and failure to obey.

La Règle. Quoted by Bremond, op. cit., vol. ii, p. 123.

ECKHART

People should think less about what they ought to do and more about what they ought to be. If only their being were good, their works would shine forth brightly. Do not imagine that you can ground your salvation upon actions, it must rest on what you are.

Quoted by Huxley, op. cit., p. 186.

WILLIAM TEMPLE

The proper relation in thought between prayer and conduct is not that conduct is supremely important and prayer may help it, but that prayer is supremely important and conduct tests it.

Christus Veritas, p. 45.

CHARLES DE CONDREN

Now henceforth you must perform all your works in union with the Son of God, either by feeling, intention or faith. If you have a conscious feeling of his presence, unite yourself to him through feeling. If you have none of that, unite yourself to him in intention, that is to say, try to work with the same mind and intention as he had; and if you cannot do this, then unite yourself to him in faith, that is to say, make a spiritual offering of all you do in union with his works, thus offering those as well as your own to God.

Quoted by Lear, op. cit., p. 266.

THOMAS KEN

Be not afflicted, good Philotheus, if you cannot come up exactly to the rules here given you; believe me, it was never imagined you would; it was only hoped you would endeavour it. . . . It is sincerity God requires, not perfection . . . so that your infirmities ought to humble but not discourage you.

Manual of Winchester Scholars. Quoted by Cropper, op. cit., p. 194.

W. R. INGE

In commenting on the story of Martha and Mary, those favourite types of activity and contemplation, he [Eckhart] surprises us by putting Martha first. "Mary hath *chosen* the good part; that is," he says, "she is striving to be as holy as her sister. Mary is still at school: Martha has learnt her lesson. It is better to feed the hungry than to see even such visions as St Paul saw."

Christian Mysticism, p. 161.

GIROLAMO SAVANAROLA

Accordingly, speaking of the ordinary course of the spiritual life, I say that there is need of going by the way of due means and slowly, and that perfection in the spiritual life is reached in a long time, the longer or the shorter in proportion as the grace of God aboundeth more or less, and in proportion as a man doth more or less exercise himself in good works.

Spiritual and Ascetic Letters, p. 79.

EVAGRIUS PONTICUS

The offspring of passionlessness is love; and passionlessness is the flower of active life, which in its turn consists of practice of commandments. The guardian of this practice of commandments is fear of God, which is the fruit of right belief.

Early Fathers from the Philokalia, p. 102.

JOHN TAULER

So is it with a noble-minded man. When he feels an inclination in himself to enjoy God or His heavenly grace and what is thereof, let him for a little while seek and purpose his own good, but not longer than is needful for the nourishing of his soul, that he may consume his spiritual strength again in labour; and when it has thus been spent in the noblest of all ways, from a love flowing back unto God who has inspired it, then the man must go for refreshment again into the river of life that floweth out from the throne of God, that it may again bring forth in him the fruit of good works.

"Sermon for Septuagesima Sunday". *History and life of the Rev. Dr John Tauler with 25 of his sermons*, p. 247.

GRACE

ST BERNARD

But if a man is taught or led by the Spirit, he knows that his efforts are of his own making, while it is his master and leaders that he follows; and in this way, when he comes to his destination, he can say with all sincerity: It is not I who do this, but the grace of God that works within me.

The Steps of Humility, p. 44.

God certainly is well within His rights in claiming to Himself the work of His own hands, the gifts Himself has given! How should the thing made fail to love the Maker, provided that it have from Him the power to love at all?

On the Love of God, v.

JOHN TAULER

Such a truth also receive men of which they ought not to speak at all, for the fountain of all grace and truth floweth through them, and the stream is so great that they overflow with it. This no man can know but God alone, for what God works in them goeth above all human conceptions.

The Following of Christ, vol. i, p. 127.

For all that a man doeth of himself is defective, and with that he cannot come to God. For as the creature is faulty, it worketh faulty works; and therefore if man is to come to God, he must be empty of all work and let God work alone.

Ibid., vol. ii, p. 17.

WALTER HILTON

For a blind wretched soul is so far from the clear knowing and the blessed feeling of His love through sin and frailty of the bodily kind, that it might never come to it were it not the endless mickleness of the love of God. But then because that He loveth us so mickle, therefore He giveth us His love, that is, the Holy Ghost. He is both the giver and the gift, and maketh us then by that gift for to know and love Him.

The Scale of Perfection, ch. 34.

JULIAN OF NORWICH

By three things man standeth in this life; by which three God is worshipped, and we be speeded, kept and saved.

The first is, use of man's Reason natural; the second is, common teaching of Holy Church; the third is, inward gracious working of the Holy Ghost. And these three be all of one God: God is the ground of our natural reason; and God, the teaching of Holy Church; and God is the Holy Ghost.

Revelations of Divine Love, ch. 80.

ST CATHERINE OF GENOA

But having fouled itself by original sin, it loses the gifts and graces and lies dead, nor can it rise again save by God's means. . . . Then God by another special grace raises it again, yet it stays so sullied and so turned to self that all the divine workings of which we have spoken are needed to recall it to its first state in which God created it; without them it could never get back thither.

Treatise on Purgatory, ch. 11.

WILLIAM LAW

Hence it is, that in the greatest truth, and highest reality, every stirring of the soul, every tendency of the heart towards God and goodness, is justly and necessarily ascribed to the Holy Spirit, or the grace of God.

The Spirit of Prayer, p. 30.

It is strictly true, that all man's salvation depends upon himself; and it is as strictly true that all the work of his salvation is solely the work of God in his soul. All his salvation depends upon himself, because his will-spirit has its power of motion in itself. . . .

On the other hand, nothing can create, effect, or bring forth, a birth or growth of the divine life in the soul but that light and Spirit of God, which brings forth the divine life in heaven, and all heavenly beings.

Ibid., pp. 117f.

LOVE

J. P. DE CAUSSADE

Q. What is that love of God which is termed disinterested and of pure goodwill?

A. It is that by which God is loved for Himself alone, without thought of oneself.

Q. What is interested love?

A. It is that love of Christian hope by which we love God in relation to ourselves, as our Sovereign Good and our future Sovereign Beatitude.

Q. What was the error of the new mystics on this head?

A. It was admitting Pure Love only in a certain stage of so-called perfection; whereas it may be practised even by beginners.

Q. But if this love is common to all, what difference can exist between the just and the perfect (that is, non-mystics and mystics)?

A. The difference is that the latter love God more perfectly, with the same love of pure goodwill, *since there are not two kinds of love*.

Q. But in what does this perfection of love consist?

A. To quote Bossuet, "In a more habitual, continuous, dominating exercise of the love common to all."

Q. What difference is there then between Love and Pure Love?

A. None but in degree, for all true love is so essentially disinterested that none can exist which is not pure, according to the words of St Paul: "Charity seeketh not her own."

Quoted by Bremond, op. cit., vol. ii, p. 440.

FRIEDRICH VON HÜGEL

[*On Fénelon*]

For he maintains first, that, though "in the specific act of Love, the chief of the theological virtues, it is possible to love the absolute perfection of God considered in Himself, without the addition of any motive of the promised beatitude," yet "this specific act of love, of its own nature, never excludes, and indeed most frequently includes, this same motive of beatitude." He asserts next that though, "in the highest grade of perfection amongst souls here below, deliberate acts of simply natural love of ourselves, and even supernatural acts of hope which are not commanded by love mostly cease," yet that in this "habitual state of any and every most perfect soul upon earth, the promised beatitude is desired, from the specific motive of hope of this great good, which God Himself bids us all, without exception, to hope for." And he declares finally that "there is no state of perfection in which souls enjoy an uninterrupted contemplation, or in which the powers of the soul are bound by an absolute incapacity for eliciting the discursive acts of Christian piety; nor is there a state in which they are exempted from following the laws of the Church, and executing all the orders of superiors."

The Mystical Element of Religion, vol. i, p. 69.

ST JOHN OF THE CROSS

The worth of love does not consist of high feelings, but in detachment, in patience under all trials for the sake of God whom we love.

Quoted by Huxley, op. cit., pp. 95f.

JULIAN OF NORWICH

And I saw full surely that ere God made us He loved us; which love was never slacked, nor ever shall be. And in this love He hath done all His works; and in this love He hath made all things profitable to us; and in this love our life is everlasting. In our making we had beginning; but the love wherein He made us was in Him from without beginning: in which love we have our beginning. And all this shall we see in God, without end.

Revelations of Divine Love, p. 203.

ST BERNARD

That loving God is not without its fruit and due reward; and that the human heart cannot be satisfied with earthly things.

The first degree of Love, which is the Love of Self for Self.

The Second Degree of Love, which is the Love of God for what He gives. The Third, which is the Love of God for what He is.

The Fourth Degree of Love, which is the Love even of Self only for God's sake.

Chapter headings 7, 8, 9, 10 in *On the Love of God*.

GOTTFRIED QUELL and ETHELBERT STAUFFER

What Paul means by the love of God is clear. It is the directing of God's sovereign will towards this world and its salvation. Love in action is the goal towards which God has been striving from the very beginning. . . .

God has the first word. It is he who founds the relationship. That is established once for all in Romans viii. His design, his choice, his calling—these are decisive. All that *agape* can mean proceeds from him. When men love God, that is the immediate reflection of the love which streams down from heaven upon the elect. Or rather it is an act of choice like the original act of love itself.

Love, Bible Key Words, pp. 55, 56.

ST FRANCIS DE SALES

"The best way, the shortest and easiest way of loving God with all one's heart . . . is to love Him wholly and heartily!" He would give no other answer. At last, however, the Bishop said, "There are many besides you who want me to tell them of methods, and systems, and secret ways of becoming perfect, and I can only tell them that the sole secret is a hearty love of God, and the only way of attaining that love is by loving. You learn to speak by speaking, to study by studying, to run by running, to work by working; and just so you learn to love God and man by loving. All those who think to learn in any other way deceive themselves. If you want to love God, go on loving Him more and more; never look back, press forward continually. Begin as a mere apprentice, and the very power of love will lead you on to become a master in the art. Those who have made most progress will continually press on, never believing themselves to have reached their end; for charity should go on increasing till we draw our last breath. Those who are farthest on may say with David, 'Lord, what love have I unto thy law; all the day long is my study in it;' and with the great Saint Francis, 'When shall we begin to love and serve God with all our heart, and our neighbour as ourselves?'"

Jean Pierre Camus, *Spirit of St Francis de Sales*, p. 3f.

PRESENT MOMENT

EVELYN UNDERHILL

I am sure God has something to teach us in every situation in which we are, and through every person we meet: and once we grasp that, we cease to be restless, and settle down to learn where we are.

Letters, p. 173.

J. P. DE CAUSSADE

As for the end for which I am destined, it is his business to understand how it is to be accomplished; I am as ignorant of what he is doing as of what I am destined to become; all I know is that his work is the best, and the most perfect that could be, and I receive each blow of the chisel as the most excellent thing that could happen to me, although, truth to tell, each blow, in my opinion, causes the idea of ruin, destruction, and disfigurement. But that is not my affair; content with the present moment, I think of nothing but my duty, and I endure the work of this clever master without knowing, or occupying myself about it.

Abandonment to Divine Providence, p. 58.

MEDITATION

W. H. LONGRIDGE

This . . . exercise is in form a consideration rather than a meditation, and it is intended primarily for the enlightenment of the understanding. At the same time there is no reason why it should not be reduced to the form of a meditation, or better still of several meditations, so as to appeal also to the affections and the will; and this is often the best way to deal with it in a retreat. Still our first care must always be that the understanding should be thoroughly enlightened and convinced. When that is accomplished the affections will follow, and the acts of the will will be serious and solid.

The Spiritual Exercises of St Ignatius of Loyola, p. 31.

W. H. LONGRIDGE

As we persevere in mental prayer we ought to find that we have less and less need of considerations and our prayer becomes mainly an exercise of the affections and of petitions; or in times of dryness an exercise of the will in acts of resignation and other virtues, even when we have no warm feelings in making them. And from this we may be led on to a kind of prayer which is still more simple and quiet, called the prayer of simplicity or the prayer of simple faith, a prayer which is approaching contemplation, that state in which the soul lives habitually in the presence of God, not by any effort of the imagination, but by love and the union of our will with the will of God.

Retreats for Priests, pp. 302f.

KENNETH E. KIRK

The Christian life is *not so much a life of following rules, as a life of following Christ*. "Character", said F. W. H. Myers, "is largely a resultant of the direction and persistence of voluntary attention"; and the Christian character can in no way better be formed than by acts of attention concentrated upon our Lord.

Some Principles of Moral Theology, p. 131.

LORENZO SCUPOLI

In meditation do not so tie thyself down to certain points, that thou wilt meditate upon none other; but wherever thou shalt find rest, there stop and enjoy the Lord, at whatever step of the way

He shall be pleased to communicate Himself to thee. And though thou omit what thou hadst laid down, have no scruple; for the sole end of these exercises is to enjoy the Lord, yet with intent not to make such enjoyment the principle end; but rather to make us love His works the more, with purpose to imitate Him as far as we can. And having found the end, we must be no longer anxious as to the means laid down for its attainment.

The Path to Paradise, ch. 7.

THOMAS MERTON

There are all kinds of techniques and methods of meditation and mental prayer, and it would be hard to begin to talk about them all. That is why I shall talk about none of them except to say that they are all good for those who can use them and everyone who can get profit out of systematic meditation should not fail to do so, as long as he is not afraid to lay the method aside and do a little thinking for himself once in a while.

Seeds of Contemplation, p. 78.

JUAN FALCONI

That wherein this exercise consists and whereon it depends is as follows. When thou canst no longer meditate upon the mysteries of Christ, or on other things, neither canst make ejaculatory prayers or exercise other affections, such as we have already described: then, since thou canst do no more, content thyself with a simple belief in this Lord, Who is God and Man. Though thou canst not picture Him in the imagination, fret not thyself for this, but see that thou believe Him as He is in Himself. Though He be in darkness, nevertheless thy soul, with dark faith, realizes that it is in the presence of its Creator and Redeemer. Persevere thou, with that faith, in His presence, knowing that thou art nothing and of no worth. Give thyself into His hands and resign thyself wholly into His fatherly will, that He may do with thee in all things and in all ways that which pleases Him, and have firm faith and confidence that He will help thee like a father and will do what is best for thee if thou place thyself in His will and art resigned thereto. Be resigned, then, and persevere, believing Him and loving Him, for this is to be in contemplation.

Straight Road to Heaven. Quoted in *Studies of the Spanish Mystics*, 1st ed., vol. ii, pp. 374f. (Rev. ed., vol. ii, p. 294.)

FRANCIS DE SALES

The bee flies from flower to flower in the spring-time, not at hazard but of set purpose, not only to be recreated in the verdant diapering of the meadows, but to gather honey; which having found, she sucks it up, and loads herself with it; then carrying it to her hive, she treats it skilfully, separating from it the wax, of which she makes comb, to store the honey for the ensuing winter. Such is the devout soul in meditation. She passes from mystery to mystery, not at random, or only to solace herself in viewing the admirable beauty of those divine objects, but deliberately and of set purpose, to find out motives of love or of some heavenly affection; and having found them she draws them to her, she relishes them, she loads herself with them, and having brought them back and put them within her heart, she lays up what she sees most useful for her advancement, by finally making resolutions suitable for the time of temptation.

Treatise on the Love of God, bk vi, ch. 2.

INNOCENT LE MASSON

Souls who are making progress in prayer, and who feel drawn to affections, should allow themselves to go to them without having recourse to reflections, save when they see that their will is altogether poured out: then they will quite gently take up their considerations. Considerations are only made in order to move the affections. Those who are drawn to affections, but make a difficulty about following their attraction because they have not made their considerations to begin with, are like those who, on finding themselves in a place, turn back again, because they have not come by the way they were told.

A Treatise on Interior Prayer, p. 30.

Authors and Works quoted

Authors and Works quoted

[Editions quoted in the text are given, where known, and dates added, when available]

AUGUSTINE OF HIPPO, St (354–430)
  The City of God. Image Books, New York, Doubleday (Eng. ed., Mayflower)
AULÉN, Gustaf
  The Faith of the Christian Church. Muhlenberg Press, Philadelphia, 1948 (Eng. ed., S.C.M., 1954)
BAKER, Augustine (1575–1641)
  Holy Wisdom. Burns Oates
BERNARD, St (1090–1153)
  On the Love of God. Mowbray, 1950
  The Steps of Humility. Mowbray, 1957
DE BÉRULLE, Pierre (1575–1629)
BOSSIS, Gabrielle (died 1950)
  LUI et Moi. Entretiens Spirituels. 7 volumes, Beauchesne, Paris, 1957
BREMOND, Henri (1855–1933)
  A Literary History of Religious Thought in France. English trans., first 3 vols., S.P.C.K., 1928, 1930, 1936
CAMUS, Jean Pierre (1584–1652)
  The Spirit of St Francis de Sales. Rivington, 1872
DE CANFELD, Benoit alias Benet CANFIELD (1563–1611)
CARTER, T. T. (1808–1901)
  Harriet Monsell
CATHERINE OF GENOA, St (1447–1510)
  Treatise on Purgatory. Sheed and Ward, 1946
DE CAUSSADE, J. P. (1693–1751)
  Abandonment to Divine Providence. Catholic Records Press, 3rd Eng. ed.

CHADWICK, Owen
John Cassian. C.U.P., 1950

CHAPMAN, John (1865–1933)
Spiritual Letters. Sheed and Ward, 1935

CLOUD OF UNKNOWING, The
Watkins, 1946

DE CONDREN, Charles (1588–1641)
Lettres. Editions du Cerf, Paris, 1943

CROPPER, Margaret
Flame touches Flame. Longmans Green, 1949

CROSS, F. L. (ed.)
The Oxford Dictionary of the Christian Church. O.U.P., 1957

DIEGO, de Estella (1524–1578)

DIONYSIUS, the Pseudo-Areopagite (circa 500)
The Mystical Theology. Shrine of Wisdom

DODDRIDGE, Philip (1702–1751)
The Rise and Progress of Religion in the Soul. Walther, 1822

DREVER, James
A Dictionary of Psychology. Penguin, 1960

DREXELIUS, Jeremy (1581–1638)
The Heliotropium. Horsey, 1889

EARLY FATHERS FROM THE PHILOKALIA
By E. Kadloubovsky tr. by G. E. H. Palmer. Faber, 1954

EASTERN CHURCHES QUARTERLY

ECKHART (c. 1260–1327)

EVAGRIUS Ponticus (346–399)

FARRER, Austin
The Freedom of the Will. Black, 1958

FÉNELON, François de S. de la M. (1651–1715)
Spiritual Letters. Rivington, 1877
Christian Perfection. Harper, 1947 (Eng. ed., H. Hamilton, 1947)

FRANCIS OF ASSISI, St (1181–1226)
Lent with St Francis. Mowbray, 1958

FRANCIS DE SALES, St (1567–1622)
Introduction to the Devout Life. Methuen, 1906
Treatise on the Love of God. Burns Oates, 6th ed.
Œuvres

GILLEMAN, Gérard, S. J.
The Primacy of Charity in Moral Theology. Burns Oates, 1959

GLEASON, R. W., and HAGMAIER, G.
Moral Problems Now. Sheed and Ward, 1960

GORODETSKY, Nadejda
St Tikhon Zadonsky. S.P.C.K., 1951

GOULBURN, E. M. (1818–1897)
Thoughts on Personal Religion. Rivington, 1875

GREGORY PALAMAS, St (c. 1296–1359)

GUILLORÉ, François (1615–1684)
Self-Renunciation. Longmans Green, 1916

GUYON, Mme (1648–1717)

HAGMAIER, G., and GLEASON, R. W.
Moral Problems Now. Sheed and Ward, 1960

HEBERT, A. G.
Preface to Agape and Eros. S.P.C.K., 1932

HEPPELL, M.
St John Climacus. The Ladder of Divine Ascent. Faber, 1959

HILTON, Walter (died 1396)
The Scale of Perfection, ed. Evelyn Underhill. Watkins, 1923

HODGSON, Leonard
Church and Sacraments in Divided Christendom. S.P.C.K., 1959

VON HÜGEL, Friedrich (1852–1925)
The Mystical Element in Religion. Dent, 1927
Selected Letters

HUXLEY, Aldous
The Perennial Philosophy. Chatto, 1946 (Fontana, 1958)

IGNATIUS LOYOLA, St (1491–1556)

ILLINGWORTH, J. R. (1848–1915)
Personality, Human and Divine. Macmillan, 1907

INGE, W. R. (1860–1954)
Christian Mysticism. Methuen, 1912
Speculum Animae. Longmans Green, 1929

ISAAC OF SYRIA, St (died c. 700)

JEANNE DE CHANTAL, St (1572–1641)

JOHN CLIMACUS, St (c. 570–649)
Ladder of Divine Ascent. Faber, 1959

JOHN OF THE CROSS, St (1543–1591)
Complete Works. Burns Oates, 1943

JUAN DE AVILA (1500–1569)

JUAN FALCONI

JULIAN OF NORWICH (died 1442)
  Revelations of Divine Love. Methuen, 1940
  A Shewing of God's Love. Ed. Anna Maria Reynolds. Longmans
  Green, 1958
KELLY, Thomas R.
  A Testament of Devotion. Hodder and Stoughton, 1957
KEN, Thomas (1637–1711)
KIERKEGAARD, Søren (1813–1855)
  Purity of Heart is to will one Thing. Harper, New York, 1946
  (Eng. ed., H. Hamilton, 1946)
KIRK, Kenneth E. (1886–1954)
  Some Principles of Moral Theology. Longmans Green, 1957
KNOWLES, David
  The English Mystical Tradition. Burns Oates, 1961
KRIVOSHEINE, Basil
  Article in *Eastern Churches Quarterly.* 1938, No. 4
LAW, William (1686–1761)
  Works. 1892
LEAR, H. L. S.
  Priestly Life in France
LEHODEY, Vitalis
  The Ways of Mental Prayer. Gill, 1917
LE MASSON, Innocent
  A Treatise on Interior Prayer. Burns Oates, 1954
LONGRIDGE, W. H.
  The Spiritual Exercises of St Ignatius of Loyola (tr. and ed.). Mow-
  bray, 1930
  Retreats for Priests. 1930
LOSSKY, Vladimir
  The Mystical Theology of the Eastern Church. Clarke, 1957
LUTHER, Martin (1483–1546)
MACKINTOSH, H. R.
  The Christian Experience of Forgiveness. Nisbet, 1944
MARK THE ASCETIC, St (c. 400)
MARQUIS, D. G., and WOODWORTH, R. S.
  Psychology: A Study of Mental Life. Methuen, 1952
MASCALL, E. L.
  Death or Dogma? S.P.C.K., 1937
MERTON, Thomas
  Seeds of Contemplation. Burns Oates, 1957
  Thoughts in Solitude. Burns Oates, 1957

MEYENDORFF, Jean
  Introduction à l'Étude de Grégoire Palamas. Seuil, Paris, 1959
MOLINOS, Miguel de (c. 1640–1697)
MONSELL, Harriet
  Life, by T. T. Carter
MORRIS, Augustine
  Straight Course to God. Faith Press, 1958
NELSON, Robert (1656–1715)
  The Practice of True Devotion. 1735
NEWMAN, J. H. (1801–1890)
NYGREN, Anders
  Agape and Eros. S.P.C.K., 1932 and 1938
OLIER, Jean-Jacques (1608–1657)
PEERS, E. Alison
  Studies of the Spanish Mystics. Sheldon, 1930 (Rev. ed., S.P.C.K.,
  vol. i, 1951, vols. ii and iii, 1960)
  Complete Works of St John of the Cross. Burns Oates, 1943
  Complete Works of St Teresa of Jesus. Sheed and Ward, 1946
PETER OF ALCANTARA (died 1562)
  Treatise on Prayer and Meditation. Burns Oates, 1926
QUELL, Gottfried, and STAUFFER, Ethelbert
  Love. Black, 1933
RAMSEY, A. M.
  The Gospel and the Catholic Church. Longmans Green, 1959
RELIGION AND ETHICS, Encyclopaedia of
  T. & T. Clarke, Edinburgh, 1908
RICHARDSON, Alan (ed.)
  A Theological Word Book of the Bible. S.C.M., 1957
ROMAINE, William (1714–1795)
  Walk of Faith
RUTHERFORD, Samuel (c. 1600–1661)
  Letters. Glasgow, 1783
SAVONAROLA, Girolamo (1452–1498)
  Spiritual and Ascetic Letters. Mowbray, 1907
SCUPOLI, Lorenzo (1530–1610)
  The Spiritual Combat and *The Path of Paradise.* Cleaver, 1847
SHERLEY-PRICE, Leo (ed. and tr.)
  Lent with St Francis. Mowbray, 1958
SMITH, R. Gregor
  Article in *A Theological Word Book of the Bible.* S.C.M., 1957

SÖDERBLOM, Nathan (1866–1931)
SPEAR OF GOLD, The
    Burns Oates, 1947
STAUFFER, Ethelbert, and QUELL, Gottfried
    Love. Black, 1933
TANQUEREY, A.
    The Spiritual Life. Belgium, 1930
TAULER, John (died 1361)
    The Following of Christ. Watkins
    History and Life of the Rev. Dr. John Tauler with 25 of his sermons.
    1857
TAYLOR, Jeremy (1613–1667)
    Holy Living. Routledge, 1879
    Liberty of Prophesying
TELFER, William
    The Forgiveness of Sins. S.C.M., 1959
TEMPLE, William (1881–1944) *Christus Veritas*. Macmillan, 1925
TERESA OF AVILA, TERESA OF JESUS, St (1515–1582)
    Complete Works. Sheed and Ward, 1946
THEOLOGIA GERMANICA
    Gollancz, 1949
THOMAS À KEMPIS, St (c. 1380–1471)
    The Imitation of Christ. O.U.P., 1949
THOMAS AQUINAS, St (c. 1225–1274)
    Summa Theologica. Baker, 1911
THORNTON, Martin
    Pastoral Theology: A Reorientation. S.P.C.K., 1958
TOURNIER, Paul
    The Meaning of Persons. Harper, New York, 1957 (Eng. ed.,
    S.C.M., 1957)
TRAHERNE, Thomas (c. 1636–1674)
    Centuries of Meditation. Dobell, 1948
TUTE, Richard
    After Materialism What?
UNDERHILL, Evelyn (1875–1941)
    Letters. Longmans Green, 1943
WEIL, Simone
    Waiting on God. Fontana, 1959
WHITEHOUSE, W. A.
    Article in *A Theological Word Book of the Bible*. S.C.M., 1957

WHITTEMORE, Alan
Psychology reinforced by religion. Holy Cross, New York
WHOLE DUTY OF MAN, The. 1742
WILBERFORCE, William (1759–1833)
A Practical View of the Prevailing Religious System of Professed Christians. Edinburgh
WISE, Carroll A.
Pastoral Counseling. Harper, New York, 1951 (Eng. ed., H. Hamilton, 1951)
WOODWORTH, R. S., and MARQUIS, D. G.
Psychology: A study of mental life. Methuen, 1952

Index

Index